Young Children
in a
Computerized
Environment

The *Journal of Children in Contemporary Society* series:

- *Young Children in a Computerized Environment*
- *Primary Prevention for Children & Families*
- *The Puzzling Child: From Recognition to Treatment*
- *Children of Exceptional Parents*
- *Childhood Depression*

Young Children in a Computerized Environment

Mary Frank, MS in Education, Editor

Volume 14, Number 1, Fall 1981
Journal of Children
in Contemporary Society

The Haworth Press
New York

The Journal of Children in Contemporary Society: Advances in Theory and Applied Research is a refereed, quarterly, interdisciplinary journal which focuses on contemporary educational, psychological, social, medical, political, and economic issues that are currently influencing the growth and development of young children. The diversification of the themes and the collection of theme-related articles that are timeless, theoretical, pragmatic, and written by noted professionals make this journal of value to those training teachers; to child care workers; to clinicians; to those organizing in-service training programs; to those administering various child-related agencies and institutions; and to those developing contextual material for scholarly papers, journals, and textbooks.

This journal is published in the Fall, Winter, Spring, and Summer of each year. Articles in this journal are selectively indexed or abstracted in: *Cumulative Index to Nursing and Allied Health*; *Exceptional Child Education Abstracts*; *Resources in Education*; and *Ulrich's International Directory*.

Journal of Children in Contemporary Society was originally published by the Pittsburgh Association for the Education for Young Children (formerly the Pittsburgh Area Preschool Association) under the title *Children in Contemporary Society*.

Journal of Children in Contemporary Society is partially sponsored by Carnegie-Mellon University Child Care Center, 1060 Morewood Avenue, Pittsburgh, PA 15213.

MANUSCRIPTS should be submitted in triplicate to Mary Frank, Editor, *Journal of Children in Contemporary Society*, 427 Olympia Road, Pittsburgh, PA 15211. All editorial inquiries should be directed to the Editor.

BUSINESS OFFICE. All subscription and advertising inquiries should be directed to The Haworth Press, 28 East 22 Street, New York, NY 10010: telephone (212) 228-2800.

SUBSCRIPTIONS are on an academic year, per volume basis only. Payment must be made in U.S. or Canadian funds only. $24.00 individuals, $36.00 institutions, and $48.00 libraries. Postage and handling: U.S. orders, add $1.75; Canadian orders, add $6.00 U.S. currency or $6.50 Canadian currency. Foreign rates: individuals, add $20.00; institutions, add $30.00; libraries, add $40.00 (includes postage and handling).

CHANGE OF ADDRESS. Please notify the Subscription Department, The Haworth Press, 28 East 22 Street, New York, NY 10010 of address changes. Please allow six weeks for processing; include old and new addresses, including both zip codes.

Library of Congress Cataloging in Publication Data
Main entry under title:

Young children in a computerized environment.

(Journal of children in contemporary society ; v. 14, no. 1)
Includes bibliographical references.
1. Computer–assisted instruction. 2. Children and computers.
I. Frank, Mary (Mary Isabelle) II. Series.
LB1028.5.Y67   372.13'9445   81-20028
ISBN 0-86656-108-0   AACR2

Young Children
in a Computerized Environment

Journal of Children in Contemporary Society
Volume 14, Number 1, Fall 1981

IMPACT OF COMPUTER TECHNOLOGY ON THE CHILD IN A
   NARCISSISTIC CULTURE
Computer-Based Education in the Age of Narcissism
   John E. Searles

INTRODUCTION

Journal of Children in Contemporary Society is a quarterly journal that has been published by the Pittsburgh Area Preschool Association for the past 13 years. During that time it gained national and international recognition among various professionals, various professional agencies, and various professional associations which dedicate their services to young children because its primary goal has been to publish a thematic journal which identifies societal issues which are presently influencing the growth and development of young children.

This issue, which is the first to be published by The Haworth Press, Inc., will continue to address itself to the societal issues, as well as the related practitioner-oriented problems, and the practical strategies which are presently having an impact or will have an impact on young children.

The theme for this issue, "Young Children in a Computerized Environment," has been selected because the rapid technological advances in computer technology and the reduction of costs for computer equipment have brought about a proliferation of computers which are now being used around the world for education purposes as well as for scientific, business, and military purposes. Thus, it is timely to become more knowledgeable about the influence the computer will impact on our total global society.

The implications of living in a computerized environment for many professionals, for many parents, and for many children are still unthinkable and still incomprehensible. However, for educators it is becoming clear that computer technology is providing the means for amassing more data which will ultimately be influential in promoting revolutionary changes within the traditional education system. Obviously, computer technology is here to stay, and much like the TV era, it

Journal of Children in Contemporary Society, Vol. 14(1), Fall 1981

is predicted to be the precursor of positive and negative influences on the total world population.

Since there is a dearth of literature in reference to the impact of computerization on young children, the editorial staff has made a serious attempt to identify the present aspects of computer technology which directly relate to this area of concern. This includes a technological-philosophical overview, a discussion of the impact on education, readings on the integral relationship between research and the industries which are producing and marketing the hardware, and questioning the value of computerization in yet another culture in which we live —the culture of Narcissism. Because we are on the frontier of a new era, there are other perceivable issues that will occur, such as the new role and responsibilities of the teacher in the classroom, the predicted changes in the ways in which individuals will process information, and the impact information technology will have on traditional family life styles, traditional school systems as well as its total impact on society. Only time, more research, and the sharing of practical experiences will provide us with perspectives on and solutions to these issues.

We are, indeed, appreciative to those who contributed papers to this issue. It is hoped their efforts will be instrumental in developing even more sophisticated knowledge on the impact of computer technology on all young children all around the world.

MIF

PHILOSOPHICAL OVERVIEW

TECHNOLOGY IN THE EDUCATION OF YOUNG CHILDREN

Russell A. Dusewicz, PhD

ABSTRACT. In a labor room within the maternity ward of a modern hospital, a young mother-to-be awaits the birth of her first child. Beside her is a machine which monitors the heartbeat of the fetus to assure that all is going well. Across town an aged stroke victim, in rehabilitation, sits in front of a special video screen and responds to questions and material projected on the screen in a programmed manner. In another neighborhood, a toddler gets up in the wee hours of the morning, runs out to the living room, turns on the color TV and watches the brightly colored lines and the soft humming noise, for it is too early for the morning's cartoons. Later the toddler is joined by his not-much-older sister, and they tune in "Sesame Street" while their parents catch a few extra moments of sleep. In a nearby elementary school, students are using hand calculators in place of paper and pencils to solve problems requiring addition, subtraction, multiplication, and division.

From birth to old age, in the home and in the school, technology is having a profound impact upon how we live and how we learn.

Technology in Education

Since the debut of O. K. Moore's "Talking Typewriter" in 1963, machines and technology have been assuming an ever-increasing role in the formal education process of our increasingly technological society.

Russell A. Dusewicz is Director of Evaluation and Child Studies, Research for Better Schools, Inc., 444 North Third Street, Philadelphia, PA 19123.

Journal of Children in Contemporary Society, Vol. 14(1), Fall 1981
©1982 The Haworth Press

Educational technology has been variously defined and is generally taken to represent that collection of knowledge related to the application of the science of teaching and learning to the real world of the classroom, together with the tools and methodologies developed to assist these applications. It is these tools and methodologies that are of particular concern here. Principal among these tools of learning are television (and television-related technologies), film, audiotape, radio, programmed instruction, and computers.

Television

Television technology includes not only educational programs broadcast via the standard TV, but also video cassettes, videodiscs, closed circuit broadcasts, cable transmission, and satellite transmission, among other forms. In the normal use of television, the signal which appears on the face of the TV set is generated by an electronic camera in the television studio. The resulting information is processed electronically by equipment in the transmitting station and sent via radio waves to the television viewer's set. In addition to the transmission of live broadcasts, television technology has the capability of recording and playback on magnetic tape, disc, film, or other suitable medium. The capability of storage and playback provides the potential for flexibility and access comparable to the printed page. Exemplary programs and speakers can be videotaped and stored for later use by teachers in classroom instruction. It also makes possible some rather unique applications of television technology to education such as the "electric report card." This consists of videotaping student daily performances in math, reading, and other areas and then showing the tapes to parents with appropriate commentary at report card time (Lehane, 1978). Closed circuit broadcasts are direct electronic transmissions of signals not broadcast via over-the-air radio waves. These may be used for observation of classrooms in one part of a school by visitors gathered in another room, without disturbing the classroom itself. Closed circuit TV is also useful in situations in which a demonstration is being conducted in one classroom with a limited set of equipment, and it is desired that it be observed by children in a number of other classrooms. Cable TV is another alternative means of transmission to over-the-air radio wave broadcasting of television signals. Cable transmission has a greater channel capacity and is not influenced by external conditions and interference. Cable TV is being used more and more extensively for educational broadcasts and is being exploited for access to computer systems such as TICCIT (Time-shared Interactive, Computer-Controlled, Information Television). Satellite transmission, the sending of television signals from one point on the earth to another via satellites, today is a common occurrence. This capability of television technology has been utilized for educational programs broadcast in the Rocky Mountain States, Alaska, Appalachia, and in other isolated rural areas where access to central educational facilities and schools is limited. It has also been used extensively in many other countries throughout the world.

Television has a profound effect upon the education of children today, especially at the younger age levels. The creation of "Sesame Street" and "The Electric Company" by the Children's Television Workshop has provided an infusion of the teaching-learning process into the home. These programs as well as more recently developed efforts, such as "Picturepages" (Dusewicz & Coller, 1979), have served to provide an early exposure to the structured learning process and to integrate learning in the home with learning in the school or preschool environment.

Film

Film technology in education principally involves the use of 16 mm, 8 mm, and Super 8 mm formats. These are used in both reel-to-reel and cartridge forms and in both front and back projection modes. In their application to education, both television and film technology overlap considerably. However, because of its greater optical freedom and variety provided by film type and processing, only film has been able to bring certain visual effects and imagery and experiences not presently possible in other media. Film libraries and film use are abundant among school districts across the nation. Significant efforts are currently ongoing in linking film technology with television and computer technologies in new ways.

Audiotape and Radio

Audiotape technology has found its most extensive use in areas of education which are primarily aural. These include music and languages. The advent of cassettes and portable tape recorder-players has added a new dimension to this area of technology. Audiotapes have also been combined with filmstrips or slide sequences to enhance, through audio commentary, their meaning and impact.

Radio technology and its educational application in the U.S. has been limited since the advent of television. Although educational programs may be found in both AM and FM broadcasting, the special situations or purposes in which radio technology can be maximally effective in education have not been sufficiently investigated. Uses of radio technology for education purposes have been more frequent in western Europe, in the Outback of Australia, and in developing countries, where it has been utilized to achieve educational gains as a low-cost alternative to television.

Programmed Instruction

Programmed instruction technology was originally conceived in the 1920s by Sidney Pressey as consisting of a self-instructional device in which test material was presented to the student and which gave the student information on whether or not the correct answer had been selected. Later, in the 1950s B. F. Skinner significantly advanced this notion with his ideas on teaching and his experiments with operant conditioning. Like Pressey, Skinner emphasized the need for the learner's individual control of his rate of progress and active participation in the learning process (Skinner, 1968). Skinner went a step further, however, with his belief that learning could take place wholly through self-instruction without the use of other materials. Skinner also believed that student errors should be eliminated as much as possible and thus advised structuring programs in a linear fashion where small units of material were presented to the learner, each followed by a question requiring a response and each response followed by a reinforcement in the form of an affirmation or correction of the student response. Norman Crowder, believing errors were useful pieces of information in the learning process, developed the concept of branching programming as an alternative to the linear approach. In branching, the sequence of small units depended upon the type of answer given by the student. A correct answer might permit the student to skip ahead several units or frames, while various incorrect answers might direct the student to different remedial branches of the program. During the 1950s and 1960s many differential mechanical and electromechanical machines were developed to present programmed instructional material. Even books were formatted to present such programs in a linear or branching fashion. The utilization of increasingly complex branching programs came into greater use with the unique capabilities inherent in the developing area of computer technology.

Computers

Computer technology has had and continues to have a significant impact on our educational system and the way we learn both within and outside of that system. All computers, whether of the large mainframe variety or at the mini or the micro level are comprised of three functionally different elements: a central processing unit, a memory unit, and an input-output system. The central processing unit or CPU represents the arithmetic-logic and controller functions. It is this unit that directs the actions of all elements of the computer and performs arithmetic-logical manipulations. The memory unit is that component in which data, information, and instructions are stored for use in processing operations. This memory may be of several types: fast access internal core memory or peripheral memory such as disc, drum, tape, or a similar medium. The input-output system is that combination or configuration of equipment by which data, information, and instructions are entered into the computer and the results of processing are taken out of the computer. Input-output vehicles may consist of punched cards or punched paper tape readers, magnetic tape readers, optical scanners, keyboards, remote data units, computer terminals, or other similar devices.

In order to utilize the vast capabilities of the computer, the prospective user must be able to communicate with the machine in a manner which best suits the intended use. It is for this reason that various computer or programming languages have been developed. FORTRAN (Formula Translation) is most appropriate for science and engineering applications, COBOL (Common Business Oriented Language) is widely used in business, and BASIC (Beginners All-Purpose Symbolic Instructional Code), developed initially to introduce students to the use of computers, is generally suitable for a wide variety of applications. COURSEWRITER and TUTOR are languages which were developed for use by the teacher in writing tutorial programs. LOGO and FOCAL have been shown to be suitable for use by elementary school students in designing their own programs. Many other languages also exist.

A popular form of use of computer technology in education has become the application of an input-output device known as a terminal to connect the user to the computer in an interactive fashion. In recent years, increasingly sophisticated TV-like cathode ray tube (CRT) terminals have dominated the market. These will undoubtedly be replaced in the future by yet more sophisticated visual display mechanisms. Large computer systems used for instructional purposes (such as the PLATO system) and employing terminals of these types can each service several thousand students.

Other, more specialized, applications of computer technology in education have been developed for the handicapped learner. One example is the Kurzweil Reading Machine for the Blind, which converts ordinary printed materials into spoken synthetic speech. Parallel efforts to convert speech to print for use of the deaf are in the experimental stages. These as well as other devices, such as the

"OPTACON" which translates print into tactile impulses and the "Speech Plus" talking calculator, serve as communication aids in facilitating the learning process for handicapped children and adults.

Computer-Based Education

Microelectronics and computer technology are affecting all levels of education today and will have an even more profound impact on how children learn in the years ahead. Sophisticated input devices will allow the spoken word, a handwritten symbol, a touch on a display screen, or the movement of a control stick to provide information to a computer and activate processing operations by even the youngest of children. Tiny inexpensive computers and related microelectronic devices may well replace the paper and pencil as the principal student tools in the classroom.

A major impetus toward adapting computer technology to the education system today has been the movement toward individualization of instruction as the preferred mode of conducting the education process. Early attempts at individualizing instruction met with limited success due to the inadequacy of resources available to apply to meeting the objectives of the program and the cumbersome and localized methods for implementing the individualization process. Among the most promising and successful of such programs have been: Individually Prescribed Instruction developed and marketed by The Learning Research and Development Center at University of Pittsburgh and Research for Better Schools, Inc. and Individually Guided Education developed by the Wisconsin Research and Development Center for Cognitive Learning at the University of Wisconsin.

The teacher's ability to effectively handle large amounts of information, to monitor the progress of students, and to provide optimal instructional objectives is essential to the functioning of such programs. The application of computer technology to the individualization of instruction issue has fostered a symbiotic relationship leading to the growth in development and application of both movements.

The broad advance in application of computer technology in the field of education may be partitioned into three principal areas: Computer-Based Resource Units (CBRU), Computer-Managed Instruction (CMI), and Computer-Assisted Instruction (CAI).

Computer-Based Resource Units

Computer-Based Resource Units are computer-produced collections of suggested instructional objectives, content items, activities, materials, and tests designed to provide teaching ideas focusing on a specific topic or area of interest. Teachers generally use the ideas and suggestions in planning their work in the classroom. The units are designed to save time and effort for the teacher and at the same time provide a greater match of teaching resources to the needs and interests of the students in the class. The CBRU is also intended as an aid in the individualization of instruction. Computer suggestions may be made sensitive to student interests and goals, student characteristics, and the educational philosophy and approach of the teacher. Based on all relevant information, the computer generates a resource guide containing instructional objectives, content outlines, suggestions for large and small group activities, instructional materials, tests, and individualized activities. In the end result, however, the teacher must make all final decisions with regard to specifically what portions of the computer-generated resource guide suggestions should be implemented in the classroom.

The use of Computer-Based Resource Units in the classroom is initiated by, and dependent upon, the role of the teacher as a decision maker and curriculum planner. CBRUs rely upon teachers for development, analysis, and improvement. They cannot be developed without the aid of teachers; the coding of items for retrieval as well as the actual programming and format of the resource unit guide require teacher input and review.

The CBRU concept has been applied at the elementary and secondary levels in education in a wide variety of subject areas, including the basic skills, science, history, and even environmental education (e.g., Dusewicz, 1975). It has also been employed at the college level and in areas applicable to exceptional education situations.

Computer-Managed Instruction

One of the early forms of computer application to education has been that of Computer-Managed Instruction. This application of computer technology generally refers to use of the computer by the teacher as a supplementary tool for the purpose of: managing the schedule or activities of a student as that student progresses through a program of instruction, testing the student's mastery of the material presented, and determining an appropriate tutoring plan for students having difficulty with the material presented. Thus, using CMI, a student may be given a diagnostic test and on the basis of the results of this test be directed to library materials, specific books, audiovisual materials, or a CAI lesson. CMI has been increasingly applied in educational situations where emphasis has been placed on individualizing instruction, using competency-based learning, and increasing basic skills through individualized educational planning. One such effort was the development and operation in the 1960s of the Pennsylvania Retrieval of Information for Mathematics Education System (PRIMES). This teacher-oriented computerized retrieval system consisted of a lesson-by-lesson analysis of all basal mathematics programs (K-6) by content, expected pupil behavior, and problem type among other variables. By using this system, a teacher could design a math curriculum with activities and test materials to suit the particular characteristics, strengths, and weaknesses of the students to be taught (Dusewicz, 1976).

Currently, computer-assisted testing, computer-generated test materials as well as computer-based guidance and counseling systems are but a few of the many variations of the application of CMI to the education process.

A major comprehensive application of CMI has been in connection with the Individually Guided Education model, resulting in the Wisconsin System for Instructional Management (Belt & West, 1976). The principal function of this system is to improve decision making relative to the instructional program of a school, leading to maximum educational benefits for each student while making efficient use of all available human, material, and financial resources. The system provides for three major decision areas and six basic processes or functions. The decision areas include: specification of performance expectations, identification of instructional needs, and selection of appropriate instructional experiences and settings. The processes involve: testing, scoring, performance profiling, diagnosing, guiding/managing the instructional program, and instructing. This system of Computer-Managed Instruction has the capacity to retain records of the utilization and effectiveness of instructional activities, equipment, space, and sequencing of related objectives, and thus provides a means for self-evaluation, further development, and improvement.

Computer-Assisted Instruction

Computer-Assisted Instruction, as contrasted with Computer-Managed Instruction, generally refers to interactions between the student and the computer for the purpose of learning. CAI is a method of instruction in which a student is generally in direct communication with a computer by means of a terminal in the form of a typewriter or a display screen and keyboard. In a CAI system, information is presented to the student, student responses are communicated to and processed by the computer, and feedback is provided to the student. The computer, through its programming, maintains a certain degree of control over the material presented to the student and may present different material depending on the nature of the previous response given by the student. While in CMI the teacher or other members of the instructional staff are the recipients of information from the computer in order that they may manage the instructional process, in CAI the student is the recpient of information given by the computer. Thus, in CMI, the teacher makes decisions on instructional management based on computer-provided information, in contrast to CAI in which the computer manages the course of instruction based on its internal programming and the types of responses received from interaction with the student.[1]

Functionally there are three primary types of uses to which CAI is generally applied: drill and practice, tutorial, and dialogue. The drill and practice function is the simplest and most widely used. Its purpose is to complement instruction provided by a teacher and to render immediate feedback on student responses. Drill and practice routines are generally factual in nature and highly rigid in format and demands. Tutoring routines utilizing CAI involve the presentation of new information to the student in a systematic fashion with branching opportunities employed in accordance with the manner in which the student responds to prior questions. The dialogue function is the most complex level of CAI, involving direct communication between the student and the computer. In this instance, new material is presented to the student. However, unlike the former functions, the student is able to ask questions, give responses, and request additional information. Following this approach, instructional robots have been created with the capability of communicating verbally with students. Utilizing a variety of CAI programs, these robots are able to work with elementary school students at their own ability levels and adjust the difficulty of instructions to match the level of functioning of the individual students.

The first uses of CAI were employed by firms in the computer industry in the late 1950s to train their own personnel. Early experiments in CAI at Stanford University, the University of Illinois, Brigham Young University, and the University of Texas, as well as other schools, colleges, and universities throughout the nation, contributed to the current state of development of CAI. These experiments produced thousands of curriculum materials and programs in many subject areas and at many grade levels. One of the earliest of these

---

[1] It should be noted that this distinction between CAI and CMI is somewhat blurred in several current systems of computer-based education which offer combinations of both CAI and CMI features.

experiments, the PLATO (Programmed Logic for Automatic Teaching Operations) project, first began at the University of Illinois in 1959. This project was continued under joint sponsorship of Control Data Corporation and the National Science Foundation. One of the earliest and largest CAI users was the Chicago Public School System which placed a CAI system in its ghetto schools in 1970 to teach reading and math. A year later, a central computer and 105 terminals connecting 32 elementary schools were available. It is important to note that PLATO has had a great impact on CAI development due to the sharing of ideas and materials, the related research conducted and the groundwork it broke for the next generation of CAI developers and users. This was the beginning of the PLATO system which today delivers interactive CAI material of the latest and most sophisticated type to thousands of school children across the nation. In 1972, the MITRE Corporation in conjunction with Brigham Young University and the National Science Foundation began development and field-testing of TICCIT, the Time-shared Interactive Computer-Controlled Information Television system of CAI. The purpose of this effort was to use microcomputer and television technology to create and deliver CAI lessons and educational programs to community college students.

With increased use of computer-assisted instruction at the elementary levels, more and more interest was generated toward application of CAI for beginning instruction in the basic skills. One such program, involving the teaching of beginning reading, was the PLATO Elementary Reading Curriculum project (PERC) at the University of Illinois (Yeager, 1977). PERC lessons are designed for first graders. PERC uses computer terminals with a touch-sensitive display screen. From the outset, students are taught that they are in control of the computer. In the first lesson, "Freddy Frog," students are told that they can make the frog hop by touching it. When they find out they really can make "Freddy" hop to wherever they touch on the screen, they know then they really are in control of the terminal. Other examples, more instructional in nature, include "Animal Maker" and "The Race." The former lesson, "Animal Maker," provides an opportunity for students to create their own exotic and unique animals while learning sight-words. They are able to put two words together, such as alligator and hippo, and the computer then shows them what an alligator-hippo would look like. This lesson not only permits the practicing of sight words, but also prepares students for the notion of compound words and generally instills in them some idea of the power of words. The latter lesson, "The Race," exemplifies a unique use of the computer for teaching reading via branching stories. A dog and a cat argue about who is faster and agree to have a race to settle the question. The students decide how fast each one is to run, the route to be run, and the positioning of obstacles in the race. The computer then conducts the race just as the students constructed it.

Today, CAI systems and programs are in use at all levels of the educational system from preschool and first grade to postsecondary instruction. Their application is no longer confined to the school, but is readily available in conjunction with microcomputers marketed for use in the home. Such companies as Radio Shack, Texas Instruments, Commodore, Apple, Atari, Magnavox, and others provide video games and learning packages consistent with the CAI approach. Thousands of preschool and elementary school children are already "doodling" electronically, in color, on their home TV sets using video games.

Many times that number are playing assorted learning games on hand-held calculators such as "Dataman," "Speak & Spell," the "Little Professor," or interacting with "2-XL," a talking robot which asks questions, plays games, tells jokes, recites riddles, plays music, and sings. Still others are learning complex rules and developing rapid reaction skills to the various computerized sports games available in the form of electronic baseball, football, soccer, hockey, basketball, racing, etc. The application of computer technology of these types both in the school and in the home at present appears almost limitless.

A Glimpse at the Future

Somewhere beyond the present lies a future characterized by vast changes in the way we live and the way we learn as a result of the incessant advance of technology. We are clearly at a technological juncture in which the manual and mechanical are rapidly giving way to the electronic and the magnetic.

It is interesting to note that during the next 20 or so years, the first generation of teachers who have never known a world without television and computers will be taking control of the education system. The kind of perspective with which these teachers approach the education of children will be distinctly different from their predecessors. For the field of education, this is of tremendous import; for it is these individuals who will be employing, in the teaching-learning process, the technologies of the future.

The linking of the various other technologies with computer-based education will serve to create a highly sophisticated learning system of the future, portable enough to be suitable for use in both school and home.

The increasing miniaturization of equipment, or what has been called microelectronics, has already led to technological developments such as the portapak video camera, the video cassette, and electronic films. These new films may eventually lead to a television camera only half inch square and a hand-held, battery-operated computer. It is conceivable that within the next decade, such tiny portable computers will be as readily available as hand calculators are now and as inexpensive. Students of all types and ages will then be able to own and carry about a computer with capabilities that most school districts cannot afford today.

REFERENCES

Belt, S. L., & West, S. F. Implementing individually guided education (IGE) with computer assistance. *Educational Technology*, September 1976, 40-43.

Dusewicz, R. A. *Environmental education computer based resource unit evaluation.* Harrisburg, PA: Pennsylvania Department of Education, 1975.

Dusewicz, R. A. *An evaluation of the transfer of PRIMES.* Harrisburg, PA: Pennsylvania Department of Education, 1976.

Dusewicz, R. A., & Coller, A. R. *An evaluation of the picturepages program.* Philadelphia, PA: Research for Better Schools, Inc., 1979.

Harnack, R. S. Ten years later: Research and development on computer based resource units. *Educational Technology,* November 1976, 7-13.

Lehane, S. The electric report card. *Educational Technology*, June 1978, 32-34.

Skinner, B. F. *The technology of teaching.* New York: Appleton-Century-Crofts, 1968.

Yeager, R. F. *The reading machine.* A paper presented at the Annual Meeting of the International Reading Association, Miami, FL, 1977.

POSITIVE AND NEGATIVE USES OF TECHNOLOGY IN HUMAN INTERACTIONS

Ethel Marie Tittnich, MS
Nancy Brown, MS

ABSTRACT. Technological advances and current changes in the family and society have the potential to create individuals capable of widespread destruction, without the desire or capacity to control these impulses.

The authors examine the history of current trends and place the children they have observed in the context of a society which looks to technology to save us from ourselves rather than developing human resources in order to have technology serve positive human needs.

Educators, families, social policy makers, and technologists are presented with a challenge to alter these trends.

Introduction

The launch of the Russian satellite Sputnik in the late 1950s plummeted the United States into the space race. The resulting technological explosion related to the storage, processing, and retrieval of information reflected the concern over the cold war and the space race of the military-industrial complex. The technology of that time was developed as a means to an end—to lead this country into space and military supremacy. More recently, however, there has evolved a

Ethel Marie Tittnich is Adjunct Assistant Professor, Department of Child Development and Child Care, School of Health Related Professions, University of Pittsburgh, Pittsburgh, PA 15261. Nancy Brown is a Child Development Consultant.

Journal of Children in Contemporary Society, Vol. 14(1), Fall 1981

period of relative quiescence in the space and arms race, and developers of technology, in their search for other applications, have entered into the social sciences.

Now we are faced with another dilemma —how to use the technology available to man's social/humanistic advantage, how to manage the large store of information as a social/humanistic resource, and how to transmit knowledge about the use of technology, and the knowledge itself, to young children. There has been a tendency, coupled with the concern for technological supremacy, to use technological models and methods to deal with educational and human needs.

Granted, technology and the use of technology have many advantages and have evolved in many ways to make life easier, to increase the quality of life, and to free time for other purposes including creative and social endeavors. However, technology has also interfered with the quality of life as evidenced by concern over the environment and nuclear weapons. But more importantly, technology has the capability of interfering with a person's creative endeavors and his/her social relationships. What will be the impact of tomorrow's technology on today's children? We need to take stock of where our past decisions have brought us.

Objections to technological advances are often based on the contention that man's use of technologies creates unnatural conditions in his environment, in cultural conditions, or in the human organism itself. Creating is natural for humans; thinking is natural for humans. The consequences of man's creations are sometimes positive and sometimes negative. Certainly destructive devices created for military use are capable of snuffing out humankind, but not all technology has a sinister meaning for human development and interpersonal growth. People with speech handicaps can communicate more effectively with the aid of computerized devices; society has been and will continue to be enriched with the expanded knowledge of our solar system brought about through space technology; technical advances in the field of medicine offer hope to those suffering from disease and handicaps.

However, even those devices that we tend to think of as bringing us closer to one another may have the opposite effect given the right set of human conditions. Technical advances in communication permit us to talk with one another over long distances. However, most people are aware that it is easier to tell someone off over the telephone than it is face to face. Writing a nasty letter is even easier. Distance between people lessens the impact of the other person's reactions and reduces the guilt felt by individuals who normally behave in a socially responsible way. Similarly, the same technology that allows us to travel rapidly over great distances in order to be together is also a means of separating individuals and of avoiding being too close to one another. Technology enables us to act in social isolation.

In order to assess how useful technology will be to us in enhancing the quality of life we must look at the potential for technology in the context of the human social framework. Will man develop the capability to subordinate technology to his own creative, constructive end, or will the capabilities of technology be developed as an end in itself, with a resultant potential for destructiveness, not only in a physical sense, but also in a psychological, creative, and interpersonal sense?

Technological Potential

Until now, technology has been accessible to persons in a few well-defined areas such as science and the military. It is predicted, however, that in the rather immediate future the cost of this technology will decrease so that it will be available to almost everyone. To many, the attractiveness of the computer lies in the promise of eliminating human error. Computers are best at doing repetitive work over and over with unfailing accuracy and great speed. They are capable of storing vast quantities of information and are very good at keeping secrets. Computers can direct machines in making perfectly patterned carpets, can direct railroad cars to the correct destination, and can separate air traffic.

However, computers are incapable of dealing with ambiguity and dual meanings. Using computers to select a mate overlooks the fact that human relationships are seldom concrete and unambiguous. That people wish they were, and attempt to make relationships fit this technological system, says something about the people in our society and what they want for themselves from others. The no-risk, no-commitment value system that pervades our society and the tendency to interpose technology into human interactions, should it continue into subsequent generations, do not augur well for humankind, given the technological capabilities that we already have.

The possibility already exists for the erosion of privacy through satellite spying, data collection on individuals through television opinion pools, and other computerized information in schools, banks, and hospitals. What kinds of information will be stored? How will it be used? One has to consider the nature (or potential nature) of the person who will be using this technology. In doing so, one must first consider the impact of the current social situation on the development of our children.

Human Potential: Emotional Development

Currently, in this country we are experiencing many rapidly changing social phenomena. There is increased mobility; the number of single
parent families is increasing; and an increase in the number of working
mothers is resulting in an increase in the number of young children who
receive care outside the home. While there are parents who have no
option but to place their children in group care, more and more parents,
following trends which stress self-fulfillment and self-gratification,
elect group care in order to devote time to personal goals.

The way we care for our children is changing, almost certainly
altering the kinds of people who will be the creators, consumers, and
decision makers in the use of the new technology in the near future.
Specifically, how do personal life changes in a rapidly changing
environment and a potentially fragmented life experience impact on a
young child's development?

Based on the authors' observations in day care, children who
experience an inordinate number of changes and disruptive life experiences often exhibit a lack of cognitive constancy —which is the realization that a stable world exists apart from themselves and remains
unchanged. The child has no point of reference in time or space. For
these children, there is a lack of connectedness from one event to
another. Every experience is isolated from every other experience, and
they are all unrelated to the child or his actions. Life to this child is a
series of nonsequential images to be accepted passively and unques-
tioningly or to be acted upon by a discharge of physical energy or
aggression, but it is not to be understood.

The cognitive implications, of course, are that the child who lacks
cognitive constancy is unable to take in information and then process
it. He/she cannot make discriminations and comparisons; he/she
cannot see relationships of cause-effect, figure-ground, and classifica-
tion. He/she cannot begin to organize time and space without it, and
he/she cannot maintain a mental image of an object, leading to further
difficulties at the level of symbolic representation.

Emotionally, cognitive constancy is a prerequisite to psychic separation from the mother —mother cannot exist apart from the child unless
he/she can imagine her stable existence in another place. Therefore,
the child who lacks cognitive constancy and yet must separate from
mother is not able to cope effectively with the separation.

Another common characteristic of these day care children is their
"object hunger." Object hungry children reach out indiscriminately to
any adult who happens to be nearby. According to one consultant,
"This is a child who in one minute is on your lap, in your hair, running

cars up your arm. When I walk into classrooms, I can almost pick out three or four . . . That's a big percentage." There seems to be no end to the emotional hunger of these children. They are bottomless cups who constantly seek emotional filling. The behavior observed in these children is a by-product of the society in which they and their families live.

However, regardless of the quality of personnel in day care or the life experiences of the child, going from home care to day care is a profound change for any child. Children are expected to adapt, and most of the time they do adapt—but not without giving up something, for adaptation means the child must give up old perceptions, expectations, or sets of behavior in favor of those that fit the new set of circumstances. Also giving shape to the adaptive behavior will be the child's needs—not only physical needs but emotional ones as well.

How children adapt depends on the individual temperament of the child. Some defend themselves from the pain of separation by denying their dependent needs in an attempt to avoid childhood altogether with its attendant vulnerabilities. The "who needs you" attitude and lack of warmth in many children are their way of coping with the feeling that significant adults are inconstant and undependable. "There's never a parent around when you need one."

Day care children exhibit a variety of behaviors which lead the authors to conclude that day care is not an innocuous experience for children as they are affected profoundly, perhaps permanently, in their relationships with people. As more and more children are placed in group care, the greater the impact it is likely to have on society as these children take their places in the adult world.

Educational Trends

The historical roots of today's educational trends are also found in the launching of Sputnik and the furor it caused in the educational community at that time. Old methodologies were questioned, and new methodologies were found wanting. Ever since then, there has been a growing trend to view the use of technology as a methodological answer to education, knowledge, and informational needs.

Prepackaged educational programs, intended to eliminate the risk and uncertainty about what the child was getting, have proliferated with the content ranging from math to emotional-social development. Adults identified with the form but not the substance of caring for children. Caregivers working with preschool children were taught classroom management skills, neglecting the deeper level of understanding children. An irritating array of canned phrases and teaching gimmicks could be observed in the behavior of those professionals working with children: "We're all friends." "We all share." "I'm not angry with you; I'm angry with what you did." "Use your indoor voice." —as though learning these phrases insured that the adult was doing the right thing and was communicating to the child the information he/she was supposed to learn. Silencing and attention getting signals such as flicking lights off and on, piano chording, and zipping lips were the "soft technologies" that provided the teacher with "remote control" of the children. Overlooked was an understanding of what the particular child needed. When the adult's words or skills did not fit what the child needed, there was a breakdown in the adult's ability to cope with behavior.

Using computer data to assess educational achievement is an extension of the trend to look less at children with all of their rich, and sometimes mystifying contradictions, and rather settle for an artificially flat profile prepared by a dispassionate machine which cannot process subtle human interactions as well as another human being can. One educator defended the use of prepackaged educational materials and electronic teaching machines because she did not trust people to teach children. People have a tendency to be influenced by their feelings when teaching children, and she cited a number of destructive examples. Machines, on the other hand, were "accurate, fair, and nonpunitive," she said. That this educator overlooked the value and moral necessity of learning taking place in a human context is a frightening prospect. In fact, no person has machine-like consistency when it comes to human interactions.

Children, on the other hand, are extremely gratified by the responsiveness of a machine when they touch a button or turn a knob. It heightens the sense of being in control and comforts the child with its predictability. Like the educator, children who have found the significant adult in their lives to be unresponsive to their needs and their cues may withdraw from interpersonal confrontation and turn to machines for gratification, essentially giving up on humans.

Conclusion

Fascinated with each new technical gadget, we have supported the growth of technology with our attention and with our resources and have placed in technology our hopes for survival and society's advancement. Simultaneously we have allowed the areas of human understanding and development to remain in comparative ignorance and neglect, offering meager support during the best of times and withdrawing resources when budgets must be cut. Children are the most consistent losers in this hierarchy of values.

Technology has outstripped our abilities to deal with it. Adults with infantile social and emotional responsibility have the capacity to hold society hostage because they have at their disposal sophisticated technical devices that can wreak widespread destruction and havoc.

It is time then, to look to the development of people —those who will decide how the computer is programmed and what uses we will make of technology. The obligation for responsible social and moral uses of technology must come from the individuals who develop and use it because the technology itself does not possess those human characteristics.

SUGGESTED READINGS

Ballard, W. W. The rise and fall of humanity. In M. Smart & R. C. Smart (Eds.), *Infants: Development and relationships*, 2nd ed. New York: Macmillan, 1978.

Boulding, K. Science: Our common heritage. *Science*, February 1980, *207*(4433).

Henderson, M. M. Technology's help in putting information to work. *Bulletin of the American Society for Information Science*, 1979, *6*(1).

Huxley, A. *Brave new world*. New York: Time Inc., 1946.

Lasch, C. *The culture of narcissism*. New York: W. W. Norton, 1978.

THE IMPACT OF TECHNOLOGY ON THE ETHICAL DEVELOPMENT OF CHILDREN

John J. Fetterman, STL, MA, MLS

Prologue

I have been asked to write a paper on the impact of technology on the ethical development of children. I think it is proper for me to indicate at the outset of my areas of competence, at least in an academic sense, and also my areas of incompetence. By training and practice I am a theologian, a classicist, and an information scientist. I know relatively little about the developmental psychology of children outside of the experience of participating in the growth of our four particular ones with my wife Kate.

My view of ethics is strongly influenced by my Judeo-Christian background. By this I mean to take as a premise the creation of the world and man by God, the responsibility of men for each other and the world, and a linear and purposeful sense of history. Ethics implies people and choices and not necessarily things. Things (e.g., technology) do not inherently have any ethical dimension. The capacity of technology to do a good or a bad act is a function imposed on it from the outside by some human agent.

As far as children go, I do know that they are strongly influenced by the attitudes and examples of their elders as well as their peers. To a large degree, my children's ethical frame of reference about technology,

John J. Fetterman is Vice-President for Consulting, American Micrographics, 485 Union Trust Building, Pittsburgh, PA 15219. He is also an Episcopal priest of the Diocese of Pittsburgh and is now serving as Interim Rector of Christ Episcopal Church.

Journal of Children in Contemporary Society, Vol. 14(1), Fall 1981

from cars to computers, is an expression of my own attitude about things being a means to an end and not an end in themselves. With technology as simple as a pen, men have dealt out life and death, love and hate, truth and lies. The pen, in and of itself, has no ethical dimension and neither does the computer nor lasers nor nuclear fission.

The rest of this paper will deal with attitudes about the use of technology which may be helpful to some of you in the formation of children. I enter this discussion with a strong sense that no one controls the destiny of each other. Our children come to us with so much already started in their genetic and biological structure and then have so many influences from peers and the rest of the world that parents and teachers have a relatively small amount of time to form the offspring of their bodies and minds.

A Classical Viewpoint

The myths of ancient Greece are psychic archetypes and as such are often times helpful in understanding attitudes and the human condition. In the beautiful work of the *Theogony*, Hesiod tells us that when the Olympian gods wanted to make men they entrusted the task to Prometheus (i.e., forethought) and his brother Epimetheus (i.e., afterthought). Epimetheus started first with the animals. Since the gift of immortality already belonged exclusively to the Olympian gods he decided to give the animals the strength and swiftness and courage and shrewd cunning, fur, feathers, wings and shells and the like —until no good was left for men. There was no protective covering and no quality to make them a match for the beasts. Too late, as always, Epimetheus was sorry and asked his brother's help. Prometheus, then, took over the task of creation and thought out a way to make mankind superior. Prometheus fashioned upright, like the gods, and then went to the sun where he lit a torch and brought down fire. For the Greeks, this is a unique gift and glory of man and the means for his superiority over the animals. Hesiod writes: "And now, though feeble and short-lived / Mankind has flaming fire and therefrom / Learns many crafts [i.e., technology]."

With your indulgence, I would like to offer an interpretation of this myth. Technology is proper and essential to man. It is proper by reason of man's intelligence (versus instinct in animals) and essential, at least in a relative sense, for man's fulfillment and survival. It enables man to build on the basic strengths inherent to him and to develop himself to his fullest potential. Even with simple machines, like the fulcrum and the lever, the inclined plane, and the wheel, man vastly increases his own strength and speed so that he is more than he was without these devices.

It is precisely the development of technology that is one of the inherent differences between man and animals. This may sound like a truism, but I suspect there are some who feel, at least subconsciously, that technology is the bane of man's existence. I am suggesting that this is as proper and essential to man as speech. Take either away and you have something much less than man at his best.

Early on in the development of technology, concerned individuals began to seek legislation for its proper use. Hammurabi in his famous code has a passage in which he decrees that if a builder builds a house and it falls down and kills somebody, the builder shall be killed. A bit excessive you might say, but the point is well made. D. Milesk-Pytel (1979) cites another code established by Dr. Vivian Weil of the Illinois Institute of Technology whereby she has designed a course for graduate engineers in which she prods them to consider the consequences of their technological designs and applications. She structures the course to present three kinds of problems: (1) relations with other engineers as in cases of competition bidding and advertising, (2) relations with a boss as in the disclosure of defects, (3) relations of technology to society as in cases of pollution.

The course seems to be designed to get at some very basic issues in the use of technology in a way that will make engineers consider the consequences of their designs before their houses fall on people. It seems to me like the kind of social responsibility that could be introduced into discussions as early as high school years in terms of work on products that may turn out to be defective or even harmful to people.

The Technological Dilemma

Modern man, like Moses struck dead on the threshold of the Promised Land, has learned to master nature with technology only to run the risk of being banished from it. For classical theology nothing stands more in need of salvation than natural man. But technology, for all its capacity to enhance and enrich man, is impotent to save man from the devils that lie within him. Technological man is prey to abundance —albeit deceptive and disfiguring. Never has abundance been so aware of its own contradiction and futility. The problems of poverty, disease, and environmental decay cannot be solved merely by the use of more and more technology. In fact, technological magic is not much better than primitive magic in dealing with the fundamental issues of human existence, and, in addition, it is much more destructive.

Technology seems to have its own momentum and its own futility. It seems to me that we need to rear children who are competent in technology and sensitive to the needs of others. Are there creative people among our teachers who can formulate games or write stories that will develop the ethical imagination of children around computers and nuclear power in addition to bean stalks, bears, and dwarfs?

There is much good that can be attributed to the modern state of science. Rene Dubos (1972) in his stimulating book *A God Within* (the literal meaning of enthusiasm) says that science is evolving from the description of concrete objects to the study of systems and the interdependence of the whole cosmos upon each of its parts. We have learned that the fundamental law of ecology is that everything is relevant to everything else. We may be about to recapture an experience of harmony in the universe that is truly an intimation of the divine. In science classes we may teach our children about the interdependence of natural systems and in literature about John Donne's "No man is an island." It is the same truth wrapped up in a different package.

The Postindustrial Society

Since Professor Daniel Bell of Harvard coined that marvelous phrase describing our society, the concept has become very useful in helping us to understand who we are and what we are all about. A postindustrial society like ours is one in which more than 50% of the GNP is provided by the information-processing industry. We have been this way for several decades now. Russia, Germany, and Japan are still obviously industrial societies and the so-called developing countries are still agrarian societies. My reason for introducing this point is to say that the proper development of children in any society is a function of their learning how to use the tools of that society. In an agrarian society, they are farm implements; in an industrial society, manufacturing machinery; in the postindustrial society, the computer. I want to spend the rest of the paper talking about the computer as teacher and tool and then draw some conclusions about its impact on our culture.

PLATO Was My Teacher

One of the easier ways of learning how to use the computer as the tool of the postindustrial society is through Computer-Aided Instruction (CAI). This technique first came to prominence in the early 1960s when Control Data Corporation and the University of Illinois began a joint project. The result of the collaboration has been an efficient and easy to use language called PLATO (Programmed Logic for Automatic Teaching Operation). PLATO is now in its fourth generation and provides a time-sharing, interactive, full graphics system of instruction to about 800 institutions. One of the other elementary tools of our culture, television, has been successfully joined to CAI in work done by the MITRE Corporation and Brigham Young University dating from the early 1970s. Developments over the past several years have made possible the production of first minicomputers and now microcomputers. As a teaching tool these microcomputers have several advantages over older and larger time-sharing systems. They are portable, relatively inexpensive, and small enough not to threaten the novice user.

Richard Simonds (1980) points out that nothing is quite so meaningful in terms of learning psychology as having entered a program with "bugs" only to have it spew out some kind of nonsense. The instant reinforcement provided by a computer seems better than having work returned a few weeks later.

CAI and microcomputers teach both content (i.e., languages, mathematics) and technique. It seems to me that it is critical to teach students how to learn with such tools as computers. We cannot teach them all the facts about anything, only the technique of learning. Along with doing that, we can raise their level of consciousness of to how to use that information in our society.

Epilogue

Children learn by doing and by example. As they grow to take their place in a complex technological society they should be taught as early as possible how to use the tools of our culture for their own happiness, growth, and the benefit of others. I am suggesting both the formation of attitudes and technical competence. Ignorance of technology can only make people apprehensive, fearful, and vulnerable. The art of living within large systems can teach children a powerful lesson about interdependence, sharing, and the unity of the world. I think this is a strong foundation for any ethical system.

REFERENCES

Dubos, R. *A god within*. New York: Charles Scribner's Sons, 1972.

Milesk-Pytel, D. With a dose of morality. *American Education*, 1979, *15*(1), 31-36.

Simonds, R. An overview of computer graphics in education and training. *Computer Graphics World*, 1980, *3*(3), 32-38.

THE IMPACT OF COMPUTER TECHNOLOGY ON EDUCATION

COMPUTER-BASED EDUCATION (CBE): TOMORROW'S TRADITIONAL SYSTEM

Peter J. Rizza, Jr., PhD

ABSTRACT. The article examines the role of computer technology in the educational process and discusses some of the major reasons for the slow evolution of Computer-Based Education (CBE). It also describes the functions CBE technology can perform in delivering and supporting the learning process. It goes on to describe several major challenges which education faces and suggests some ways in which CBE may be able to meet and resolve these challenges.

Three barriers to the widespread use of CBE are presented, and specific responsibilities are laid out for education, government, and business in their interdependent roles in support of high-quality education.

The article closes by noting that the use of CBE technology in education is not a question of whether it should be used but rather how soon it is destined to become the traditional education of tomorrow.

Introduction

The purpose of this article is to examine the role of computer technology in education. To do this, it is necessary to assess where society sees the introduction of new technology and to define some of the basic aspects of Computer-Based Education (CBE). This paper will identify several major challenges facing education and give some examples of how CBE is being used to help respond to these challenges. Finally, this article will examine three major barriers to the introduction of CBE into the schools and spell out the corresponding responsibilities of these barriers.

Peter J. Rizza is a Senior Educational Consultant, Education Technology Center, Control Data Corporation, P.O. Box 0, Minneapolis, MN 55440.

Journal of Children in Contemporary Society, Vol. 14(1), Fall 1981
© 1982 The Haworth Press

How Do We Use Technology?

It is generally accepted that the world is moving quickly into the technological age. High technology is permeating all aspects of society and is affecting our lives continuously. The advances made in technology can be seen in the use and application of telecommunication, satellites, pay-by-phone banking, hand calculators, and digital toys, just to name a few. Business and industry are constantly introducing various forms of new technology to take advantage of cost-effective, high-quality support systems in building, assembling, maintaining, and distributing their products.

Most people would not think of going to a bank which had all transactions done by hand—it would simply take too long and be constantly fraught with errors. It has been estimated that if the largest bank in California had not adopted computers to process daily transactions, every man, woman, and child in the state would have to work for the bank in order to process the volume of business it currently sustains. Even the automobile (which replaced the horse and buggy) is getting a new face lift with electronic ignition, microprocessors, and solid state equipment. Local mechanics are being retrained in maintenance practices to perform digital tune-ups and generate computerized diagnostics.

Major scientific breakthroughs have been highly dependent upon advancements in technology. The medical profession has enjoyed a tremendous growth rate in the numbers and type of services which can be administered daily to patients. This is in direct correlation to the applications of technology in solving medical problems and assisting hospital staff. The thought of going to a medical center which refuses to use advanced diagnostic equipment would be out of the question if you lived near any well-equipped hospital.

Where, then, is education in this technological revolution? The one area where technology holds the greatest hope for impact is ironically the one area where the potential of technology is being applied the least. In a recent report in *People and Computers*, conducted by the Educational Development Center (EDC) of Boston, it was noted that it appears inevitable that computers will have a major impact on education. Congress stressed last year, in a subcommittee report from the House Committee on Science and Technology entitled "Computers and the Learning Society," that the new information handling technologies—computers in particular—can have important effects on the practice of education at all levels. Virtually everyone who has written on the question agrees that the potential is enormous. EDC has noted that historically the introduction of new technologies to education has been disappointing. Attempts to redefine educational practices to take advantage of liberating technologies have been met with endorsement but not with adoption. Educators appear to have a deep-set skepticism toward anything that plugs into the wall. EDC concluded that the question now is not whether computers will find a place in education but how.

The reason that many educators have not taken a more aggressive role in introducing CBE technology is because they do not understand what the computer can and cannot do. They are not familiar enough with CBE applications to see where it can help the most. Concerns over dehumanized education, cost of education, and the fear of job replacement by machines are more symptoms of the lack of understanding rather than causes for not introducing CBE in schools. However, before we discuss the barriers to using CBE in schools, it may prove beneficial to review what is meant by computer-based education. This next section presents a brief summary description of the different forms of CBE.

What Is Computer-Based Education (CBE)?

Computer-Based Education encompasses the wide variety of computer applications which play either a direct or indirect role in the educational process. A distinction should be made at this point that CBE has little to do with computer science instruction or computer literacy. Computer science is simply one more content area for CBE application, much the same as mathematics, French, or music. In order to describe the types of applications of the computer to instruction, it is convenient to think of three educational functions the computer can perform. The computer can be the teacher of new material, the manager of student learning or the aid to the learner in acquiring new skills.

1. The Computer as the Teacher

In this function, usually referred to as Computer-Assisted Instruction (CAI), the computer aids in the delivery of instruction. The most common use of CAI has been at the lowest level of interaction between the student and the computer, namely, drill and practice. The ability to provide extensive practice of newly acquired skills in a timely mannner on an individual basis via a computer has proven very effective. Some CAI programs require students not only to practice but actually to apply new skills in a variety of embodiments. This type of applied practice increases retention and transfer of learning. Another form of CAI takes on the tremendous responsibility of providing tutorial instruction on new skills. While this is not the most sophisticated use of the technology, it is by far the most difficult to accomplish effectively. The CAI tutorial lessons must present sufficient material in an interesting way to allow students to master the designated objectives. In addition, good tutorials allow for a number of branching points for review or remediation, and more clever ones actually adapt the instructional paradigm to the learner's cognitive style. Probably ths least used type of CAI lessons are simulations. These lessons actually simulate real experiences for learners by requiring them to apply the newly acquired skills on a continuous basis. In this mode, students actually create unique problems which can be solved in a wide variety of ways. Collectively, via the use of tutorials, drill and practice, applications and simulations, the computer can aid in the delivery of individualized instruction to students in a flexible, broad, and effective manner.

2. The Computer as the Learning Manager

In this function, usually referred to as Computer-Managed Instruction (CMI), the computer aids in the management tasks associated with the instructional process. The computer applications which fall into this category are designed to help educators better manage the learning process. To this end, numerous CMI systems have been developed. According to Dr. Michael Allen, a principal consultant for Control Data, a complete CMI system must provide; (1) a testing system which includes scoring and analysis capabilities, (2) a functional gradebook which provides students and instructors with performance feedback, and (3) analytical capabilities which recommend the learning experiences likely to be most effective in helping the student attain mastery and which report on the general effectiveness of the instructional materials the instructor is using.

It stands to reason that the CMI system, which retrieves reliable test items, scores students' responses, and grades performance, would be useful to most educators. Some CMI systems have the ability to tailor tests to a specific student level and terminate tests when enough information has been collected for proper assessment of student performance. Record keeping is nothing more than the collection of data, something for which computers were originally designed. Educators have found that easily accessible, up-to-date student records are extremely helpful in improving the instructional experience. The capability of the computer to provide learners with proper learning activity assignments is another CMI application. This is a complex decision and requires the CMI system to match up specific student needs with appropriate learning materials. If the concept of individualized instruction is to be implemented with a reasonable expectation that educators will be able to manage the testing, record keeping, and prescription decisions required for effective learning, a CMI system is necessary.

3. The Computer as a Learning Aid

In this function, usually referred to as Computer-Supported Learning Aids (CSLA), the computer aids in the expansion of the human intellect or capability as a tool to the learner during instruction. The computer can be used to perform a number of specific applications which will increase the learner's ability to comprehend a subject which could not be undertaken otherwise. Subjects, like numerical analysis, require large complex computations to be performed in order to let the student actually comprehend the subject matter. For example, knowledge of how to use the computer for statistical analysis is one of the most requested computer applications for a wide variety of subjects ranging from psychology to structural engineering. Other application packages, such as business modeling programs, financial problem solving, utilities and graphical analysis, allow students to readily learn about concepts, which would have been too difficult to undertake because of prohibitive computational requirements. The computer can be used to actually expand or augment the intellectual capability of its user. By presenting analysis of large aggregates of data in "real time," the computer can allow for the investigation of concepts too cumbersome to study otherwise.

By now you should have an initial feel for the different educational capabilities of the computer. Each educational system will have to decide which CBE functions or combination of functions show the greatest promise to help it address its specific educational needs. To solve a very focused specific problem, it is possible that a limited system will be the best choice. To solve a wide variety of needs, it is possible that a more comprehensive system which can provide all three functions would be best. Before we examine what CBE system features are needed, we should look at what educational challenges exist which must be addressed by CBE technology.

What Are The Challenges Of Education And How Can CBE Application Help To Address Them?

There are many challenges in education which require attention by society. Some of these cry out to be solved by the use of one or more forms of CBE.

1. Individualized Instruction

Before a learner can take part in an individualized program, a thorough diagnostic assessment of the learner's characteristics and capabilities must be conducted and analysed. If each student is to learn individually, specific learning material must be made available at the right time and delivered at a pace commensurate with the learner's ability. For a teacher to accomplish this for one student is extremely difficult; for a teacher to accomplish this for a classroom of 30 students is impossible without some form of CBE system support. All CMI features are required for the management of an individualized system, and most CAI features are necessary for the individualized delivery of instructional materials. Patrick Suppes of Stanford University once noted that the most important aspect of computerized instructional devices is that the kind of individualized instruction, one made possible only for a few members of the aristocracy, can now be made available to all students at all levels of abilities. Certainly, if individualized instruction is to be realized, the computer will play a major role.

2. Multilingual Education

With the increasing number of people in the United States demanding to be taught in their native languages, the school systems are being heavily taxed to respond. In the State of California, depending on student population, the law requires schools to deliver instruction in any of 30 different languages. It would be impossible to have a single teacher deliver multilingual instruction to several groups of students concurrently. On the other hand, a CBE system would have the capability of delivering this instruction provided the course materials were available in the proper languages.

3. Remedial Education

There is a great need to provide remedial education in schools today. Because of the increased emphasis on individualized student achievements measured by each state on local minimum competency exams, schools are struggling with the accountability question in education. There is a major cry for remedial programs which teach students the fundamental basic skills needed to be functionally literate in our society. While the current activity is focused around reading and math skills, these programs will expand to cover a wider variety of skills. The delivery of basic skills instruction can be done effectively through the use of the computer where diagnostic assessments can be performed continually and meaningful instruction can be given at the appropriate level for each and every student in a comprehensive educational package. In the State of Florida, a CBE basic math skills package was delivered in three communities via the Control Data PLATO system. The results were so positive that the program was expanded to nine new sites the following year. Success was measured by the Florida Statewide Minimum Competency Mathematics Exam.

4. Gifted Education

This population is the least served of all students in schools today. Schools should accommodate the need of each gifted child even if it is a class of one student. No longer can gifted students in small or poor school districts be deprived of a stimulating education. The concept of equal access to quality education programs is just now coming into focus in education. Advanced students need to be able to access challenging instructional materials in a wide variety of disciplines. Only a computer system which has access to a wide scope of quality instructional materials provides equal access to quality education regardless of the student's geographic or socioeconomic location.

5. Special Education

This area of education holds the greatest potential for the impact of CBE systems on the educational process. The new responsibilities placed on schools by laws like Public Law 94-142 at the federal level requires all schools to generate an Individualized Educational Plan (IEP) for every special education student. Furthermore, the schools are legally bound to deliver all services deemed necessary in the IEP in a "least restrictive environment." The need to keep progress records on all special education students and deliver the prescribed type of learning materials identified in the IEP requires the type of management system and flexible delivery system which CBE offers. Some states, like Massachusetts, have a mainstreaming law which places special education students into the regular classroom. The teachers of the regular classroom have had no training in handling the special needs of these students. The aid of a CBE system to diagnose, prescribe, and monitor student progress is essential to the delivery of individualized instruction tailored to the special student's needs and abilities.

6. Continuing Education

This area of education is growing rapidly. As more adults realize that career changes are needed, they will call upon the school system to help prepare them for new jobs. Learning will be expanded from a limited 12-year system to one of continuous, life-long learning. The school system will have to respond with individualized, self-paced education in a larger number of disciplines with a low-cost delivery system. As Alvin Toffler noted in *The Third Wave*, over the long pull, we can expect education to change. More learning will occur outside, rather than inside, the classroom. Instead of rigid age segregation, young and old will mingle. Education will become more interpersonal and interwoven with work and more spread out over a lifetime. Computers will be a major instrument for this change.

What Are the Barriers to Widespread Use of CBE in the Schools?

John Dunworth, President of Peabody College, once noted that we will not have proper education until we utilize the superb technology becoming available to us to assist in the difficult task of providing for the wide diversity that exists in every classroom. Teachers, he claims, need assistance. If technology is needed so badly, why, then, has it not been adopted widely and demanded more often? There always appear to be hundreds of reasons for using or not using technology in the classroom. Just ask any three people and you will get at least four good reasons. However, most of the reasons for not using CBE fall into three major categories.

First, the lack of understanding on the part of many educators about what CBE is and what it is not. There is always a great tendency of not getting involved with something which you do not know or understand. Teachers concerned about dehumanization of education have never seen the eyes of a remedial reading student when he has just mastered a module in a CBE reading program. Many teachers have not experienced the positive force accurate information about the learner's progress can have on both the teacher and student. Computers are tireless, consistent in quality, positive in feedback, and forgiving of student error.Most teachers know the benefit of having a wide variety of programmed materials available to students but fail to realize the potential of CBE for delivering a wide range of instructional offerings. It is now possible to teach science with biology, physics, and chemistry students in the same class or offer Latin, French, and Spanish concurrently. Educators must become more knowledgeable of CBE technology if they are going to be part of the decision-making process.

The second barrier to the widespread use of CBE is cost. Up until the last decade, the costs of the CBE systems were prohibitive, and in comparison the cost of a traditional education was much lower, but we have seen a major change in the situation since 1970. Every year the cost of technology is decreasing while the capability of the technology is ever increasing. On the other hand, the cost of traditional education (due to its labor-intensive structure) has been increasing while its capability is at best remaining the same. The 1980s will see a crossing of the cost curves when CBE instruction will be more cost-effective than traditional labor-intensive methods. Yesterday there were lengthy discussions on whether a given CBE system would be more cost-effective than the traditional approach, but I see tomorrow's discussions centering on how best to use CBE technology to solve educational problems.

The third barrier to acceptance of CBE technology is the very limited applications available on computers for educational use. Those educators with vision enough to want to use CBE in their schools often find it hard to locate adequate applications on available CBE systems. Too often, the computer vendor has only a limited set of applications to be had. In fact, the places where CBE systems are doing well are in those educational institutions where educational needs have been matched up with existing quality CBE applications. Getting schools to accept CBE systems with limited applications is similar to selling schools on the idea of textbooks and asking them to build a library with only a handful of books to put on the shelves. Furthermore, if the applications developed for use by schools do not prove to be quality products, they will not be used regardless of price or availability.

What Are the Responsibilities of Education, Government, and Business with Respect to the Future Of CBE?

In order to integrate the CBE applications into the regular educational environment, a number of commitments must be made by Education, Government, and Business. All three must work together to complement each other's strengths and capabilities to revolutionize the current educational system. Let us look at the responsbilities of each.

Education

The educational institutions have to take on the responsibility of providing a cost-effective, high quality educational process. They must accept the responsibility of being accountable to the community by delivering students who have acquired minimal competency in designated skills. The educators must take the responsbility of providing equal access to high quality educational experiences. The educators must demand that technology be introduced into the school system. Much as the medical profession has embraced new technological applications to make hospitals more responsive to patients' and doctors' needs, so should the education profession encourage use of technology to increase the school's capabilities and improve the environment for both students and teachers alike. The teacher unions should begin negotiating for computer application to reduce the amount of administrative work and increase the amount of meaningful teacher-to-student communication time. Administrators should demand that technology be applied to counter the rising cost of education. This doesn't mean the laying off of teachers to make room for computer terminals, but rather the proper mix of teacher and CBE support system to serve the existing populations not presently served. If anything, there will be a need for more teachers if CBE is used.

Dr. Michael Marcase, Superintendent of Schools for Philadelphia, expressed views about how useful technology would be for schools and how important it is for schools to take an active role in adopting CBE programs. He said he believed in technology. He advised education to look toward technology in the future and not limit their thought along one track—whether it be traditional teaching or using computers as a supplement. He also argued that technology has a future, but it must reduce the overall cost of education to be successful. The educational profession must help create environments which will allow CBE systems to be cost-effective. They can no longer force-fit computer technology into a traditional learning environment which will not support a CBE system because it has refused to adjust. Marcase thinks that school systems who refuse to adjust are doomed to failure and will be very quickly replaced by some other form of education.

Government

The federal government has two major responsibilites in the area of applying new technology to education. First, the federal government must allocate substantial sums of funds to educational institutions and businesses to cooperatively develop low-cost, high-quality CBE applications. They should identify very specific educational problems needing solutions and encourage the use of CBE applications to solve them. Note the following chart devised by Richard Carlson of Stanford Research Institute:

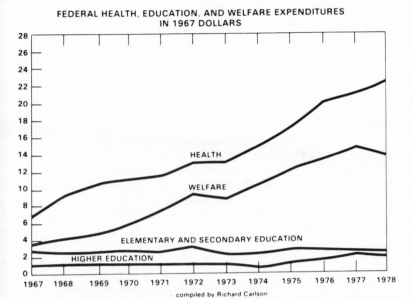

FEDERAL HEALTH, EDUCATION, AND WELFARE EXPENDITURES
IN 1967 DOLLARS

compiled by Richard Carlson
Stanford Research Institute

FIGURE 1. EXHIBIT 4: Testimony before the U.S. Senate Committee on Governmental Affairs on S991 presented October 12, 1977.

It is commendable that from 1968 to 1978 the Department of Health, Education and Welfare increased the amount of funds spent on health from $6 billion to over $22 billion and on welfare from $4 billion to over $13 billion. It is depressing to note that elementary and secondary education has remained at approximately $2 billion throughout the period. If the federal government increased the funding of education to the same level as health, cost would no longer be an issue in the development of CBE applications for schools.

Secondly, the federal government must help to introduce and to support quality CBE systems in schools. The government must continue to persevere in its attempt to provide not just special education students but all students with Individual Education Plans (IEPs). It is the right of every child to have a quality education, and the federal government is the only answer for students in low socioeconomic and deprived areas. CBE technology requirements should be attached to federal funds which go to schools in deprived areas. The federal government in all cases should strive to establish programs which can be demonstrated as cost-effective and therefore self-sustaining. Once a CBE system application has proven itself in one location, the federal government should make available start-up funds needed to replicate the system anywhere that people desire to use it. The goal is to proliferate proven cost-effective, high-quality, and self-sustaining technological advancements in education.

Dr. William Pierce, former Executive Deputy Commissioner for Support Services of the U.S. Office of Education, noted (with relationship to implementation of CBE) that he found it incredible that we Americans use the latest technological advances to their maximum in all aspects of out lives except education. He states that if we are going to appropriately release the pressure on the school system, we must take advantage of all teaching aids available to us including computers. With corresponding federal funds to support the commitment to improved education through applied technology, the goal of better cost-effective education for all may be reached.

Business

Businesses dealing in high-technology application have the responsibility to be responsive to education's particular needs. They must take a chance and invest in educational applications even though in the short term, other applications may be more lucrative and profitable. They must not continue to place education on the back burner to simmer. More joint efforts between business and educational institutions are required. The emphasis must be placed on the providing of total packages designed to solve specific educational needs. The selling of hardware alone will not be tolerated and will only set back the industry. Once businesses take the time to understand what the educator is responsible for accomplishing, they will be better able to help provide alternative solutions to major educational problems. Furthermore, business must be willing to accept the fact that if its product does not do a better job of teaching than the current system in a shorter time and at less cost, the product will be rejected by the educational community. Business must look at the total needs of a school system and help the school system apply technology in a total system's approach. Businesses must help school systems solve the many significant problems and not just small scale or limited needs. To provide these solutions at a profit to the business is to be commended, not scorned.

John W. Lacey, President of Control Data Information and Education Systems Company, stated a progressive posture which other businesses might emulate:

At Control Data Corporation we feel strongly that technology has to be part of the answer. We can add an important ingredient to what will be the effective recipe for success. In the world of the professional Educator we feel that our role is complementary and that a condition of mutual respect and cooperation must be established to bring to bear the best attributes and resources of both sectors. Alternative methods and delivery systems are available today. When blended with the experience, dedication, and human dimensions of purposeful Educators, we can effect a revolution in education that will culminate in egalitarian, high-quality, cost-effective solutions to our education problems.

What Lies Ahead?

The future will be very exciting for the application of new technologies to the concept of Computer-Based Education. The arrival of microcomputer technology, personal computers, advanced communication systems, and the videodisk all reaffirm that technology will be more a part of our everyday lives in the future. Whether they will be part of the formal educational process or not remains to be seen. Certainly if the schools do not embrace technology, the consumers will. When it becomes easier to learn something at home rather than at school, the entire educational institutional profession may collapse. It would be refreshing, though, to see educational institutions, government offices, and business working together to develop quality, low-cost educational systems. To accomplish this, however, will require creative instructional application from the educator, creative methods of funding from the government, and creative technological advancement from the businesses. One thing we do know for sure, new educational technology is coming and will be readily available. The only real question is where will you have to go to find it being utilized.

REFERENCES

Allen, M. W. Computer managed installation: A definitive design. In O. Lecarme & R. Lewis (Eds.), *Computers in education*. North-Holland Publishing Co., 1975.

Caldwell, R. M., & Rizza, P. J. *The potential and use of computer-based education in American higher education*. Paper presented at the annual meeting of the Society for Research into Higher Education, December 20-21, 1977, The University of Surrey, Guldford, Surrey, England.

Caldwell, R. M., & Rizza, P. J. A computer-based system of reading instruction for adult non-readers. *AEDS Journal*, 1979, *12*(4), 155-162.

Dunworth, J. *Seven barriers to basics*. Paper given at the School Superintendents' Seminar, November 30, 1977, published by Control Data Corporation.

Heimer, R. T., & Rizza, P. J. *Basic skills mathematics curriculum development for CBE*. Paper presented at ADCIS Annual Meeting, Dallas, TX, March 1978.

Lacey, J. W. *Control Data —The education company*. Paper given at the School Superintendents' Seminar, November 30, 1977, published by Control Data Corporation.

Marcase, M. P. *Comments from the transcript of a panel discussion on computer-based education*. School Superintendents' Seminar, November 30, 1977, published by Control Data Corporation.

Olds, H. F., Schwartz, J. L., & Willie, V. A. *People and computers: Who teaches whom?* Newton, MA: Educational Development Center, Inc., 1980.

Pierce, W. *The dilemma of choice*. Paper presented at the Chief State School Officers' Seminar, sponsored by Control Data Corporation, Minneapolis, MN, September 26, 1978.

Poore, J. H., Qualls, J. E., & Brown, B. L. *FSU Plato project —Basic skills in math for Florida high schools*. Final report, published by FSU Computing Center, Tallahassee, FL, July 1979.

Searles, J. E., & Rizza, P. J. *Computer-based education for developing educational systems*. Paper presented at ADCIS Annual Meeting, Dallas, TX, March 1978.

Suppes, P. Computer technology and the future of education. Phi Delta Kappan, April 1968, *49*, 420-423.

Toffler, A. *The third wave*. New York: Morrow, 1980.

IMPACT OF COMPUTERS
AND ELECTRONIC TECHNOLOGY
ON THE TEACHING METHODOLOGIES
AND THE LEARNING PROCESS

Glenn E. Snelbecker, PhD

What is, or may be, the impact of computers and electronic technology
on the methodologies and practices of teachers? What impact can be
expected with regard to the teaching-learning process? Ultimately,
what impact can be expected on students' educational achievement?
Will these be minor or major effects? Will they be primarily positive or
negative in character? What are some of the key issues which we should
consider when using (or planning to use) computers and other forms of
electronic technology in schools? Most importantly, how do answers to
these questions relate to the teaching of young children?

We can have a better basis for gaining answers to these questions with
regard to education in the 1980s if we have some awareness of previous
experiences with educational technology. Also helpful will be information about certain contemporary attitudes about teaching practices.

Educational Technology and Computers

Educational technology refers to the practical use of various kinds of
equipment and devices which can aid school learning, but it also includes the practical use of scientific knowledge. Thus, educational

Dr. Snelbecker is Professor, Division of Educational Psychology, College of Education,
Temple University, Philadelphia, PA 19122.

Journal of Children in Contemporary Society, Vol. 14(1), Fall 1981
© 1982 The Haworth Press

technology includes computers and electronic devices along with slide projectors and tape recorders. Educational technology also includes the research findings and the practical ideas which are needed to show how these devices can help teachers to teach and students to learn.

This broader meaning of educational technology has not always been recognized nor its significance appreciated. For example, during the 1960s there was a greater display of interest in educational technology than had been evident previously (Saettler, 1968). Some educators and psychologists in the 1960s talked and acted as though the equipment (or hardware) was most important for education. Less value was attributed to the educational content involved and to the overall school context. When some devices were developed to present information and to record the appropriateness of students' responses, some people began proclaiming that a "teaching machine revolution" had occurred. Many educators took issue with what they perceived as an attempt to replace teachers with machines. It was only somewhat later that the term *programmed instruction* gained prominence. Then it was recognized that these devices had to be considered primarily with regard to the educational content and activities which they provided, and that these educational experiences —like any others —had to be considered in the context of the total educational program (Bunderson & Faust, 1976; Snelbecker, 1974, Chapter 13).

Attitudes about the use of films and other audiovisual presentations illustrate another important point which should be recognized when considering the impact of computers and electronic technology. Many teachers seem to be hesitant, almost fearful, about the use of any kind of equipment or hardware in their classes. Various surveys have revealed a curious mix of teachers' reactions: A large majority of teachers, at best, feel uncomfortable about using equipment, while a significant minority typically comment that they do not see how one could teach without these resources. Unfortunately, many teachers have had some piece of equipment (e.g., a film projector, a tape recorder) fail during a class presentation. Such experiences make teachers even more reluctant to use *any* device with which they are unfamiliar or over which they cannot exert control.

It has frequently been observed that the teacher is a major determinant of whether a given innovation will be successful or unsuccessful in a classroom, including the nature and extent of the impact on students' learning (Hodges, Sheehan, & Carter, 1979). This appears to be true at various school levels. For example, teachers have an important role even when complex curriculum projects are implemented in schools (DeRose, Lockard, & Paldy, 1979). Also, the role of the teacher is conspicuous when innovations fail. Failures can result because teachers elect not to implement some part of the innovation, although there can also be other causes (Snelbecker, 1973).

In light of these previous experiences with educational technology, it would follow that the extent and the nature of the impact which computers may have in schools quite likely will depend on individual teachers in the classrooms. How comfortable a teacher feels about the use of computers and how clearly the teacher understands and accepts the nature of the innovation can greatly determine what kind of impact that computerized innovation will have on students.

An important step for the teacher is to become familiar with how computers function and how computers can be useful in schools. Some sources (Ball, 1972; Ball & Charp, 1978) which are oriented for younger audiences can also help adults to understand the major characteristics of computers and other related electronic devices. Sources such as the papers in this issue can inform teachers about ways in which specific computerized innovations can be used in schools.

Contemporary Views about Teacher Effectiveness

Traditionally there has been interest among teachers in finding one "best method" of teaching. Educational psychologists and other researchers have invested considerable time and money comparing one teaching method with another, usually in the hope of finding some one best teaching method which could be used in a variety of situations with different students. In that kind of context, it might seem appropriate to compare selected forms of computer-assisted instruction with other teaching methods to see which is better.

In recent years, starting mainly in the 1970s and continuing to the present, there has been growing support for a different view about teaching methods and teacher effectiveness. In brief, there is growing acceptance of the belief that there may be many good teaching methods instead of only one. There is greater emphasis on finding the strengths and weaknesses of particular teaching methods. There is support for the belief that we should examine each teaching method to identify the educational experiences they make available for students and the kinds of educational objectives for which they seem to be most appropriate. In this context, it would seem appropriate to consider the kinds of teaching-learning opportunities which can be made available via computers and other electronic devices.

A definition of educational technology was proposed by Calvin Gross over a decade ago (Hesse et al., 1967) which may help us in assessing the impact of computers in the 1980s. Gross suggested that educational technology involves "a system which is set in motion by a teacher to produce learning, and which continues to do so after the teacher removes his attention" (Hesse et al., 1967, p.l5). Gross' definition can apply to things with which teachers are comfortable and familiar as well as to computers with which teachers may feel neither comfortable nor familiar. He suggests that a teacher may "set in motion the process of education" with a textbook as well as with a computer.

Combining these ideas, it would seem important to evaluate each computer-assisted or computer-guided educational innovation to see what kind of educational process has been set in motion. Moreover, it would also seem important to consider how the particular educational process relates to other learning experiences available to students. Two other contemporary ideas about teaching practices should be noted before returning to specific qualities of computers and the experiences they make possible. First, most of the research on teacher effectiveness supports one general precept: appropriate student learning is most likely to occur with teaching methods that maximize "time on task." Stated another way, improved learning occurs when each student is constructively involved in the learning process, particularly in tasks and activities which are related to the intended learnings. Thus, if you want to help a child to learn to recognize and to use numbers, it would be wise to plan formal activities and play activities which involve recognition and use of numbers.

Second, there are certain themes which seem prominent in the instructional theories which are evolving today. Some of these theories have been developed in conjunction with computer-assisted instruction projects while others have been more directly based on studies of how people grow and learn. One emphasis is that we need to take into account the thought processes as well as the behaviors of students, recognizing developmental changes which occur throughout the lifespan. Educational activities should take these student characteristics into account. Another theme is that there should be consistency throughout the process of instruction. This involves having students (at all ages and grade levels) understand the general nature of planned activities before they start, aiding them in seeing how their activities relate to goals in evaluating their progress towards goals. For older students, this may involve rather abstract descriptions, but for pre-schoolers and early elementary students this most likely will include relating school activities to their informal play.

Potential Educational Functions of Computers

The potential educational functions of computers, as well as their implications for teaching methods and the learning process, can be considered in two ways. First, we should identify some functions which are commonly considered by designers of computer-assisted instruction. Second, we should relate these to responsibilities and activities of a classroom teacher. Of course, it should be recognized that a particular computerized innovation may involve different combinations of these functions.

The emphasis on educational technology during the past two decades has been at least partly responsible for the emergence of several theories of instruction (Reigeluth et al., 1979; Snelbecker, 1974). Common to several theories are certain steps in the process of instruction (Snelbecker, 1980): Alerting students to the intended learnings, preparing students for information to be provided, gaining and maintaining attention, presenting the subject matter and educational activities, providing for students' responses, evaluating students' progress, providing feedback to students, and keeping records of the educational activities and of the students' progress (on an individual as well as on a group basis).

Theoretically, computers can be designed to carry out all of these functions for students either on an individual or on a group basis. In practice, computer-assisted instruction and computerized educational innovations vary considerably in doing one or more of these functions. It is extremely important that teachers who may be involved in the use (or possible use) of any particular computerized innovation check to see which of these functions —wholly or in part —are handled by the computer.

The examination of the computer's educational functions ideally should be done in terms of the regular ongoing teaching-learning activities. For example, here is a list of functions which a particular computerized innovation may fulfill:

1. Diagnose a student's present educational accomplishments and needs.
2. Identify (for the student) what educational experiences and activities are available.
3. Present subject matter and activities —visual and auditory, with directions for tactile and other sensory experiences.
4. Present lessons in a fixed sequence.
5. Give students some options about what is to be learned and in what sequence.
6. Enable students to work independently at least part of the time, freeing the teacher to work with individuals or small groups of students.
7. Provide notices to the students and to the teacher when certain students need special help.
8. Provide ongoing evaluation information so that students (on an individual basis) and the teacher can be aware of educational ac-

complishments, including strengths and weaknesses.

9. Provide the teacher and the school with information about how students might be grouped periodically throughout the school year, rather than only for the beginning of the school year.
10. Provide ongoing information to the students to guide further learning, including suggestions about study habits and approaches to the learnings.
11. Enable each student to have some sense of accomplishment as identified educational objectives are attained.
12. Make suggestions to individual students about other individual and group activities which might enhance and encourage learning.
13. Provide remedial experiences.
14. Provide enrichment experiences.
15. Enable students who miss class (e.g., due to illness or other reasons) to make up work without disrupting the rest of the class.
16. Enable students to inquire about and possibly to complete educational experiences not generally available in the community school.

Issues and Information Relevant to the Use of Computers

By now it should be obvious that one cannot appropriately make judgments about all computers and their relevance for education any easier than one might make judgments about all textbooks and their relevance for education. Instead, for computers as well as for textbooks, one must take into account the attributes of a particular innovation as well as the characteristics of the local school (i.e., students, teachers, administration, community expectations, etc.).

There are, however, certain issues and ideas which need to be considered, no matter what particular innovation and local school may be involved. Similarly, there are general issues and ideas commonly explored during the process in which textbooks and other school items are selected.

Many of the issues evolve around expectations about the nature of schools and schooling. Why do schools exist? What kinds of educational experiences should be available in schools and what kinds should one have to find elsewhere? Anyone familiar with education in the United States should know that such decisions are made on a local school district level unless they involve conflicts with state or federal requirements.

As a result, for example, some communities emphasize fundamental skills, while other communities emphasize development of critical and creative thinking capabilities. While these two illustrative emphases are not necessarily inherently incompatible, professional educators and other community members typically contend that they involve competing priorities.

One issue which is especially important at the preschool level is whether there should be an emphasis on cognitive development and preparation for school or whether a preschool program should emphasize play activities and socioemotional development. Again, these need not involve incompatible emphases—since a program conceivably could have both features—but proponents of the respective views often claim that putting a high priority on one will preclude having an emphasis on the other.

A third issue concerns the roles of teachers and students in the learning process. Although there are many variations in ideas which have been expressed, a major concern is with the responsibilities of deciding what is to be learned and how. For example, some people contend that the teacher knows best both what learnings should be expected and how students best can learn. Others emphasize orienting school experiences around the natural curiosity of the student. They typically contend that the student knows best what educational objectives are personally relevant and what teaching-learning methods will be most appropriate and effective.

Discussions about the appropriateness of a given computerized innovation *or* of a textbook under consideration should take into account issues like those briefly described above. For example, an innovation which mainly provides drill and practice in mathematics skills could be useful in a wide variety of schools. However, it probably would be considered of lesser importance in schools where critical thinking and understanding of mathematics principles are emphasized than in schools where mastering fundamental skills in mathematics is given high priority. It seems likely that a computerized innovation which is designed to develop preschoolers' pre-reading or reading skills would be more compatible with a program emphasizing cognitive development than one focusing mainly on play and socioemotional development. A computerized innovation which mainly involves drill and practice would be more compatible with a teacher-controlled school program than with a school program in which students are expected to maintain major responsibilities for their learning.

How can one decide whether a given computerized innovation will be appropriate for a school? Certain kinds of consumer information are needed. Following are some illustrations:

1. What educational goals allegedly are attainable by using the particular computerized innovation?
2. What evidence, if any, is there that students actually are able to reach such educational objectives?

3. With what types of students has the computerized innovation been used?

4. In what kinds of schools and with what kinds of teachers has the innovation been used?

5. What learning processes are set in motion by the innovation? In what kinds of activities and with what types of ideas are students typically involved when using this innovation?

6. What is the rationale which underlies the particular educational objectives and the methods of instruction for this innovation?

7. With what kinds of school programs would the innovation be most compatible?

8. What are the implications for teaching practices when this innovation is used?

9. To what extent is the innovation compatible in a wide range of settings, with varying teaching practices?

10. What roles for teachers and students are important for this innovation?

11. To what extent does the innovation seem to be successful because it involves a novel approach (not necessarily a bad feature), and what provisions are there for maintaining effectiveness of the innovation once it is no longer novel?

12. What are the limitations of this innovation?

13. What kinds of problems can be expected when using this innovation?

14. What "troubleshooting" procedures are outlined for teachers and for students who use this innovation? These should include troubleshooting procedures for learning problems as well as for equipment failures.

15. To what extent might this innovation be modified so that it can become more compatible with local school requirements and needs?

16. To what extent and with what modifications might this innovation be changed to provide learning opportunities beyond those currently provided?

17. What are the major benefits and costs of using this innovation? How do these costs and benefits compare with other educational experiences?

Computers and the Education of Young Children

Thus far, the content of this paper has been relevant to educational uses of computers in general. What are some major implications for the education of young children? It seems appropriate now to consider the questions which were posed at the beginning of this paper and to relate them to the education of young children.

What is, or may be, the impact of computers and electronic technology on the methods and practices of teachers who work with young children? This primarily depends on the attributes of particular computers and electronic devices as well as on the characteristics of schools in which they would be used. One might think that only comparatively simple devices would be available for teaching young children, but there are quite complex devices and programs which have been in existence for over a decade. For example, one computer-based program has enabled preschoolers to develop their use of written language well enough that they were able to start their version of a newspaper. Some electronic devices have focused mainly on cognitive processes, while others have fostered learning of such diverse areas as recognition of musical sounds or development of social interactions in conjunction with play.

What impact can be expected on the teaching-learning process? This mainly depends on the nature of the specific computerized innovation and the characteristics of the teaching-learning processes which currently exist in the school. It is possible that some compatibility may exist, but more positive results will occur if decision makers search for innovations which either extend or enhance the current school program.

Will the impact be major or minor, and will it be positive or negative? Again, this depends to some extent on the compatibility of the innovation with the existing school program. However, even if a compatible innovation is selected, it will be necessary for the teachers and the students to be prepared to use it properly. It is quite important that adequate information be provided *before* implementation of the innovation, and it is essential that assistance be available to teachers and students when they are becoming familiar with the innovation. The more complex the innovation and the more extensive the change in the school program which will result, the greater the need for initial preparation and for ongoing assistance when the innovation is in use.

What are some key issues which we should consider when using (or planning to use) computers and other forms of electronic technology in schools? This matter already has been discussed in some detail throughout this paper. The main ideas expressed are that teachers should recognize the same issues which come up when textbooks and other school items are selected, and that it is especially important to recognize how the innovation will fit with the ongoing school program. Using computer technology in the teaching of young children involves practically the same issues and needs for information one encounters at any educational level. The young children may have some disadvantage in not being able to cope with complicated instructions and in not being able to read like older students can. However, they probably will be less intimidated than some older persons, including some teachers, when given the opportunity to try out some responsive device or fascinating piece of equipment. By the time that they have learned how to operate the new device, they will probably use it in a less self-conscious manner than will some older students.

A Final Observation

What can be concluded about the impact of computerization and electronic technology in schools? These innovations will *not* constitute a panacea for education but, if properly used, they can become extremely valuable aids to teachers and students. They can have an important positive impact not only on teaching practices and on the learning process but also on students' subsequent educational achievement.

Current research leads to the conclusion that improved learning will occur when *each* student is constructively involved in the learning process, particularly in tasks and activities which are related to the intended learnings. Given usual class sizes and conventional teaching methods, it is virtually impossible for *any* teacher—even the best teachers—to involve all students constructively in relevant learning processes throughout the school day. Computerization and electronic technology, properly selected, can aid the teacher in this regard.

In a sense, such innovations can serve as extensions of the teacher and should be viewed as such when selecting among possible alternatives and planning their use in the education of young children. They can aid in providing personalized educational experiences for each student and in giving students guidance about their progress on an individual basis in a timely fashion.

Judgments about any computerized or electronic innovation (or, for that matter, any educational innovation) should not be made in the abstract. Rather, decisions about their initial selection and about their continued use should be made with regard to particular computerized innovations in the context of the ongoing program and the local school characteristics.

REFERENCES

Ball, M. J. *What is a computer?* Boston: Houghton Mifflin, 1972.

Ball, M. J., & Charp, S. *Be a computer literate*. Morristown, NJ: Creative Computing, 1978.

Bunderson, C. V., & Faust, G. W. Programmed and computer-assisted instruction. In N. L. Gage (Ed.), *The psychology of teaching methods*. The Seventy-fifth Yearbook of the National Society for the Study of Education, Part I. Chicago: University of Chicago Press, 1976, 44-90.

DeRose, J. V., Lockard, J. D., & Paldy, L. G. The teacher is the key: A report on three NSF studies. *The Science Teacher*, April 1979, 31-37.

Hesse, Walter J. et al. The systems approach to education. *Educational Technology*, Spring 1979, 4-19.

Hodges, W. L., Sheehan, R., & Carter, H. Educational intervention: The role of follow through sponsors. *Phi Delta Kappan*, 1979, *60*, 666-669.

Reigeluth, C. M., Krathwohl, D. R., Aronson, D. T., Briggs, L. R., Scandura, J. M., Gropper, G. L., Collins, A., Landa, L., Merrill, M. D., Block, K. K., & Snelbecker, G. E. *Instructional design theories and models: Overview of their current status*. Symposium, American Psychological Association Convention, New York, NY, September 2, 1979. Book in preparation, 1980.

Saettler, P. *A history of instructional technology*. New York: McGraw-Hill, 1968.

Snelbecker, G. E. Human political and social factors in the use of educational technology to improve school productivity. In R. G. Scanlon & J. Weinberger (Eds.), *Improving productivity of school systems through educational technology. Final Report of NCET Symposium*. Philadelphia: Research for Better Schools, 1973.

Snelbecker, G. E. *Learning theory, instructional theory and psychoeducational design*. New York: McGraw-Hill, 1974.

Snelbecker, G. E. *Learning and instruction: Guidelines and rationale*. Book in preparation, 1980.

THE ROLE OF INDUSTRY AS IT RELATES TO COMPUTER PROGRAMS FOR YOUNG CHILDREN

COMPUTERS AND COMPUTER COURSEWARE: NEW DIRECTIONS FOR HELPING CHILDREN LEARN

Robert M. Caldwell, PhD

ABSTRACT. The development of the microprocessor and dramatic decreases in the cost of other computer hardware have caused a proliferation of new microcomputers and computer systems which are beginning to gain wide acceptance in schools. However, it is often confusing for educators who are unfamiliar with computers to know which systems are best for use in their schools. This article summarizes the characteristics and special features available in a broad range of mainframe, mini and microcomputer systems and discusses the applicability of each for school instruction with children. Information is also offered about hardware, instructional capabilities, courses and curricula available from computer manufacturers and publishers. The article also makes projections about the future uses of computers for instruction and their impact on schooling.

Computers are currently used in school environments for three discrete purposes: administration and data processing, instruction in how computers work and how they can be used to solve problems, and delivery of instruction in a variety of subject areas. Educators, for the most part, have readily accepted computers for the first two functions but are showing some reluctance in embracing them as legitimate means for *delivering* instruction. Many seem to be dragging their feet in

Dr. Caldwell is Associate Professor, School of Allied Health-Science Center, University of Texas, Dallas, TX 75235.

Journal of Children in Contemporary Society, Vol. 14(1), Fall 1981
©1982 The Haworth Press   55

initiating large scale programs of computer awareness, computer literacy, and computer-based instruction. Unfortunately, these educators are grossly underestimating the importance of these programs to the future of the United States.

Of nine countries, the United States ranks last in the percentage of college graduates who received a Bachelor of Science in Engineering: Bulgaria (40.4%), Czechoslovakia (32.3%), East Germany (40.1%), Hungary (47.0%), Poland (41.1%), Romania (39.7%), West Germany (37.1%), Japan (20.7%), United States (5.8%).The number of computer science graduates is growing, but at present they comprise less than 1% of total college graduates. In addition, there are nearly 10 times as many nontechnical graduates as technical graduates in the United States. This problem becomes compounded when one realizes that both the numbers of high school and college graduates are declining steadily which will serve only to reduce these percentages even further in the future. In short, the need for individuals trained in high-technology skills is critical, particularly as we plunge headlong into a technology-based future.

As educators, we can begin to solve this important problem by exposing children to computers and computer-delivered instruction at as early an age as we can. In the past, computer systems have been expensive, and their capabilities have been limited to electronic data processing. Computer systems which have been developed recently, however, are faster and more powerful than previous generations of computers and cost a fraction of what early models did. In addition, the development of low-cost microcomputers has presented almost unlimited possibilities for training future computer users. These new microcomputers are inexpensive ($500-3,000), easily transportable from classroom to classroom or from classroom to home, and require no special facilities such as air conditioning, additional electrical outlets, or telephone lines. These machines also provide features which enable them to deliver high-quality, interactive instruction on an individualized basis as well as make available an inexpensive system for teaching computer skills.

It would seem, therefore, that low-cost, efficient computer systems offer great potential for solving the problems of educating individuals in technology-related skills and for delivering information to learners whenever and wherever they might need it. The purpose of this article is to describe some of these computer systems and the unique features each offers for delivering instruction to children. It will also discuss some of the ways technology will serve us in the future and how this will impact on children who are in school now.

Because of its ease of operation and flexible, adaptive nature, it is easy to become excited about the microcomputer and its vast potential in education. However, one must not lose sight of the advantages offered by other computer systems and how they will also play an important role in the future. Large mainframe and minicomputer systems possess the ability to store and use large amounts of data, a feature which gives them a distinct advantage over microcomputers. Massive memory and instantaneous computing speed make it possible for these large systems to:

1. Store large databases on student abilities, achievement, and test scores.These data can be used effectively for:
   • Diagnosis of learner needs on an individual basis.
   • Prescription of an individualized program of studies.
   • Sophisticated record keeping and records management.
2. Evaluate student performance quickly and accurately. To provide data on the degree to which learners have mastered predetermined objectives and to aid in providing information which will improve the effectiveness and efficiency of instruction.
3. Provide multiple learning paths within lessons or within courses to an extent not possible using the more limited capacities of microprocessors.

These capabilities can provide distinct advantages for certain kinds of educational needs. It must be pointed out, however, that mainframe systems are always more expensive and require special facilities and complex telephone line communications.

A number of companies now offer excellent programs to schools through mainframe and minicomputer systems at a cost that is somewhat reasonable when one considers the elaborate computing network which that cost supports. The following is a brief description of a few of those computing systems.

Control Data PLATO

The Control Data PLATO (Programmed Logic for Automated Teaching) System was developed in 1959 at the University of Illinois. It has grown to a worldwide network of large-scale, computer-based education which supports instruction in over 100 cities in the United States, Canada, the United Kingdom, Europe, and South Africa. It provides instruction in a wide variety of topics for student populations which range from beginning readers to commercial airline pilots. With over 10,000 PLATO lessons currently available, PLATO provides one of the most comprehensive networks of computer-based education in existence. In fact, many corporations such as Bell Telephone, United Airlines, and Mobil Oil have already invested in PLATO-delivered instruction for corporate training.

The key feature of PLATO, in addition to its extensive network of terminals, is its fast response time and graphics display. Using a unique authoring system called TUTOR, an author can create lessons easily

Student receiving Basic Skills Instruction on the Control Data PLATO Learning System.

and quickly, and they can in turn be delivered at an access rate 100 times greater and an access time 1,000 times shorter than normally found with other computer storage devices. The graphics display terminal is important because it permits more than the display of mere text; graphics, animations, and other drawings are also possible (Caldwell, 1978). The PLATO system can provide dependable instruction to over 1,000 students simultaneously with the advantages mentioned above. Also, Control Data currently offers the Basic Skills Learning System, a program of computer-based learning in reading, mathematics, and language arts for grades 3 through 8 and has experienced success in helping learners realize dramatic gains in both reading and mathematics with it. (Caldwell & Rizza, 1979)

Hazeltine TICCIT

In 1971 a team of engineers and computer scientists at the MITRE Corporation and teachers and instructional psychologists at Brigham Young University worked with support from the National Science Foundation to develop the Time-shared, Interactive, Computer Controlled, Information Television (TICCIT) System. In 1976 The Hazeltine Corporation made TICCIT available commercially for educational purposes.

Like PLATO, TICCIT offers a wide variety of lessons on subjects ranging from basic skills instruction to naval flight crew training, but the instruction is offered from a much more limited access base. TICCIT will serve anywhere from 20 to 125 students (as opposed to over 1,000 for PLATO). For many school environments this number could be sufficient. TICCIT uses a minicomputer which means that the entire computer system is usually physically located at the same site where the terminals are located. PLATO, on the other hand, uses an enormous computer located in a central facility in Minneapolis, Minnesota. This on-site feature of TICCIT gives the user dedicated support for the time of installation.

TICCIT is very much like PLATO in that it offers graphics and animation capabilities, speed of operation, and a unique course development feature which allows users to develop instruction for use on-site. One feature that TICCIT offers that PLATO does not, however, is color display. The advantage of this feature to instruction may not be significant but it can be useful for cueing responses and for distinguishing features in the perceptual field of the learner. More will be said later about the use of color in instruction.

Computer Curriculum Corporation

The Computer Curriculum Corporation represents an important step in computer-based instruction in that this company offers curricula which were developed specifically for the education of young children. In 1964, with grants from the United States Office of Education, researchers at Stanford University developed programs in mathematics and reading which utilized the IBM 1800/1500. These programs were tested and proven from 1964-67 and today are delivered on a Data General Nova minicomputer which can support about 120 terminals. This computer system is usually purchased by a school district, and instruction is made available through terminals located in schools throughout the district. Computer Curriculum Corporation offers programs in basic skills, adult basic skills, GED and computer programming as well as a unique career exploration program which is based on the Department of Labor Guide for occupational exploration.

Another unique feature of this system is that every instructional site is equipped with a printer on which individualized worksheets can be generated. These worksheets can be taken home by learners for additional practice in math and reading. The exercises created on each worksheet are generated from a pool of drill items which were most frequently missed during on-line drill sequences.

TSC (Houghton Mifflin Company)

Like Computer Curriculum Corporation, TSC offers computer-based curricula in reading and mathematics skills as well as guidance information. The STRIDE reading curriculum, for example, offers 183 reading skills which are normally taught in grades 4 through 6 and adjusts reading instruction to the learner's grade level. Up to 32 students can use STRIDE at any one time, and reports and records can be provided by the system through a printer.

Neither the Computer Curriculum Corporation curricula nor the TSC curricula use graphics, animation, color and present primarily drill and practice exercises as a supplement to instruction. They contrast sharply with both the PLATO and TICCIT systems which offer full tutorial lessons illustrated liberally with graphic capabilities. An important point to be made here, however, is that none of these systems provides audio support with their lessons although all of the computer systems they use have audio capability through a variety of peripheral devices.

In summary, these large scale efforts at computer-based instruction offer the distinct advantage of instructing large numbers of learners simultaneously while recording profiles on their progress and readjust-

A Hewlett-Packard low-cost minicomputer used in many computer-assisted instruction programs.

ing the presentation of instruction accordingly. This is difficult to achieve on microprocessors although various networking configurations have been developed recently which can begin to approximate the advantages manifest in large systems. The computer curricula described above offer the additional advantage that they exist for use *now*. At present, little is available for use with microcomputers; however, the potential benefits of microcomputers, both for delivery of instruction and for developing computer programming skills are overwhelming. While they will never hope to rival the vast network of PLATO terminals which provide worldwide delivery of information, they have unique

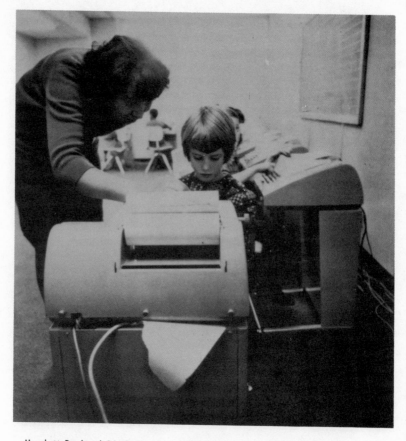

Hewlett-Packard CAI System gives individualized math drill and practice
to children in grades one through six.

features which will greatly affect the nature of schooling if not the nature of learning itself.

Without question then, the development of the microcomputer has initiated a new era for education. Their single greatest advantage, of course, is that they offer adequate computing power for most all school needs at a cost which is easily affordable. Generally, they are easy to operate and offer great flexibility in the way they can be used. Most models can be chained in a network of anywhere from 2 to 64 microcomputers and, by doing so, share the use of up to 4, 10 million-character hard disk drives. This sort of a configuration allows for most of the same advantages offered by the mainframe computer but with the added advantage of being able to disconnect any single microcomputer from the network and use it with a single floppy disk as an independent computing system. In this way, the unit can be transported to almost any location and be used for purposes which might be quite different from the purposes being served by the network. This capability will be used more in the future to allow learners to take microcomputers home and to spend additional time working on programs.

Many types of microcomputers are currently available, and in the paragraphs to follow we will look at the units which seem to have had a major impact on the market. We will compare their capabilities, advantages, disadvantages, and unique characteristics in an attempt to acquaint the reader with the various features of each. Before discussing capabilities of individual machines, however, some attention might be given to the characteristics which all microcomputers have in common.

All major microcomputers require a microprocessor unit with a keyboard, a disk drive or audiocassette player for saving and storing programs and data from computer memory, and a video monitor. (See Figure 1.)

FIGURE 1. Apple II microcomputer with game paddles, color video monitor, and floppy disk drive with diskettes.

The Microprocessor

This device is the central processing unit for any microcomputer configuration. It performs all the computing functions for the system and carries out the instructions contained in the program. It controls all aspects of the system's operation. Current models of microcomputers use either a 6502 or Z-80 processor and vary in memory capacity from 4K(thousand) to 64K characters.

Keyboard

All computers must have a keyboard which allows the user to enter data, enter programs, and enter data under control of a program.

Data Storage Devices

Data can be stored on either an audiotape or a "floppy disk," also called a diskette. Much of the reason for the emergence of inexpensive personal computers is attributable to the development of the capability of recording computer data on audiocassettes. They are inexpensive and can be used with ordinary tape recorders. Audiotape with the capacity of 30 minutes to a side can typically hold more than 100,000 characters of data. A disadvantage of audiotape, however, is that it can take from 5 to 20 minutes to record or play back a large program. Also, one cannot retrieve a particular piece of data from the tape without reading all the data which precede it on the tape. Since is is desirable to randomly access data for greater speed and efficiency of operation, the floppy disk was developed.

The floppy disk is also reasonably priced but requires a fairly expensive disk drive for operation. Most disks are 5¼" and resemble a 45 rpm record which has been inserted in a cardboard sleeve. It is made of a very thin material similar to that used for audiotape. Data are recorded in concentric circles and may hold up to 300,000 characters of data on one side. The obvious advantages of the floppy disk over audiotape are its increased storage capacity and its speed. A large program which would take 5 to 20 *minutes* to load from cassette tape can load from disk in about 5 to 30 *seconds*. For use in classrooms, this difference in time savings becomes critical. In addition, certain kinds of programs are efficient only if they are used with disk. For example, record-keeping systems, information retrieval systems, and sophisticated instructional programs require instant access.

Video Monitor

Simply put, the video monitor is usually a television which allows a user to see the results of his/her program. If your microcomputer has the capacity for color, then obviously, a color monitor is necessary. Some microcomputer systems such as the Radio Shack TRS80, the Texas Instruments 99/4, and Compucolor include video monitors of good quality with their systems.

All microcomputers also include a *terminal interface*; its function is to allow the computer to communicate with the video monitor and the keyboard. The microcomputer also has interfaces to access the audiocassette or disk drive as well as interfaces to control appliances, speech peripherals, and high speed printers. In general, any piece of equipment extraneous to the microcomputer must be linked using an interface.

With the many microcomputers available to consumers, five seem to be most popular. What follows is a general comparison of these five machines and a commentary regarding their usefulness in school environments.

Apple II

General description. The Apple II microcomputer uses a 6502 processor and offers 16K random access memory which is expandable to 32K and even 64K. Additional storage is available using either an audiocassette or single or dual disk drive. The single disk drive is the most popular for a school setting and for home use primarily because most software which has been developed by independent software manufacturers is available in diskette form. Because of the capability of the Apple II, software programs developed for it require the speed and random access capability of a disk.

The Apple II uses a video modulator which means the Apple can be connected to almost any television, either color or black and white. The video generator is capable of producing 40 characters per line and 24 lines on a single screen and can produce either 15 or six colors.

Special features. The Apple II boasts one of the fastest times for running a simple basic program. Timing results show Apple II at 40 seconds with the next closest being the Commodore Business Machines PET with 46 seconds. This is extremely fast compared with Radio Shack TRS80 (83 seconds) and Texas Instruments 99/4 (84 seconds).

The Apple offers a wide range of peripherals and can interface graphics tablets for programming graphics, videotape and videodisk recorders, speech synthesizers, printers, and variety of other devices. It has plug-ins for eight accessories including game paddles and supports a telephone coupler for communication with other similarly equipped computers.

These special features, when combined with various software utilities, produce excellent graphics and color along with animation and speech reproduction. When programmed together with well-planned instructional design, the Apple II can deliver instructional programs which will stimulate a wide range of cognitive behaviors and reinforce responses which lead to desired learning outcomes. Imagine a learning system which can diagnose learner weaknesses, adapt instruction to correct them, and individualize instruction in a way that learners can both see and hear instruction as well as respond to it. This gives us educators an extremely powerful two-way communication device which holds enormous potential for improving and truly individualizing the learning process.

Commodore Business Machines PET

General description. Like the Apple, the PET uses a 6502 processor with 8K random access memory expandable to 32K. Unlike the Apple, however, which requires plug-ins for the video monitor and disk drive, the PET includes a 9″ black and white video monitor and an audiocassette recorder self-contained within the unit itself. The video generator is capable of 40 characters per line and 25 lines per screen and can produce some interesting graphics. More recent models interface with printers and disk drives as well as telephone couplers, voice synthesizer, and additional cassette recorders.

Special features. The most distinguished features of the PET are that it is inexpensive and is relatively easy to use. Also, quite a bit of software has been developed for the PET but not to the extent that it has been for the Apple or TRS80. Beyond these features the PET offers little. It has no color and limited graphics capability; it has limited computing power when compared with Apple and has limited service outlets, an important consideration for schools where breakdowns occur more frequently with extensive use.

Radio Shack TRS-80

General description. The Radio Shack TRS-80, Model I, Level II has been an extremely popular microcomputer primarily because of its low cost (under $500). It uses a Z-80 microprocessor and offers 4K of random access memory expandable up to 16K. Its primary source of storage is an audiocassette recorder which can load into memory at a rate of 50 characters a second. It uses a black and white Radio Shack monitor which displays 64 characters on 16 lines of the screen. The TRS-80 has some well-designed graphics which are being improved on a regular basis by Radio Shack. More advanced models offer an expansion interface which is capable of an additional 32K RAM which boasts memory up to 48K. It also supports disk storage, printer, and a phone coupler (modem) to dial up time-shared systems or other TRS-80 systems.

Special features. Like the PET, the TRS-80 has gained wide acceptance because of its low cost and ease of operation. A large amount of software has been developed for the TRS-80 but it is limited without color. The software and courseware developed for this machine are probably the most extensive of all micros with Apple catching up quickly. The Dallas Independent School District, for example, has developed an entire mathematics curriculum for the TRS-80, and Radio Shack has a rather wide selection of reading curricula and games of all types.

One of the most interesting features of the TRS-80 is the speech synthesizer made for it by VOTRAX. This unit allows speech synthesis using phonetic constructions. Apple also offers a similar peripheral called the Supertalker-SD200 made by Mountain Hardware; it offers a two-way input/output speech digitizer which features speech compression to allow 100% faster transfer of words and phrases from disk.

The TRS-80 also can add voice recognition to allow the computer to respond to oral command. A final positive feature of this machine is that it has a network of Radio Shack stores for service throughout the United States.

Texas Instruments 99/4

General description. Unlike any of the previously mentioned microcomputers, the 99/4 uses a special 9900 processor produced by Texas Instruments. This machine is unique in several other ways as well. First of all, it uses a solid state module which TI calls the Command Module. This module offers 30K of read-only memory which, by the way, produces some fine color graphic capabilities in up to 16 colors. Each Command Module contains a complete, ready-to-use program on a fairly wide variety of topics. Unfortunately, the depth of these offerings is limited, and little outside of games is available for children.

The 99/4 has a total memory capacity of up to 72K. This is broken down into 16K random access memory with expansion capability to 48K, 26K internal read-only memory, and the 30K read-only memory

Texas Instruments 99/4 microcomputer.

resident in the Command Module. Additional memory can be called from a smoothly operated disk. Programs are displayed on an excellent color monitor which provides 32 characters on 16 lines per screen.

Special features. The 99/4 is unique in that it is the only microcomputer that uses an internal disk operating system. It also provides an outstanding music and sound effect capability. One of its most outstanding features, however, is a built-in Speech Synthesizer developed by Texas Instruments which duplicates the human voice in remarkable fashion. This Speech Synthesizer has already proven successful in Texas Instruments' Speak and Spell product and should prove successful in the development of programs of reading readiness and initial reading instruction.

Atari 400 and 800

General description. Both the Atari 400 and 800 represent an exciting new entry into the microcomputer market because of the great array of games and educational programs Atari has produced in the past. Both the 400 and 800 models use a 6502 processor; the 400 will only run 4K random access memory whereas the 800 can be expanded to 48K. Both models have a capacity of 32K read-only memory which is accessed from a solid state cartridge not unlike that used in the Texas Instruments 99/4. The 400 uses an audiocassette recorder for storage while the 800 uses either the audiocassette or a disk drive. In appearance, the Atari 800 most resembles an Apple II in that they both have plug-in video monitors and disk drives and have the same cream-colored cover. Like the Apple, programs are displayed over any standard color monitor, although the Atari only displays 32 characters on 16 lines. While slightly lower in price than the Apple, the Atari 800 still ranges in the $1,500 range while the 400 is competitive with the TRS-80 with the added feature of color graphics.

Special features. The really outstanding feature of the Atari product is the special color graphics and the exciting games which are being developed for it. Another capability of the Atari is a very fine voice capability which is delivered from a dual track on the audiocassette. The only problem with it is that the sound is linear, i.e. it can only be read

Texas Instruments solid state Command Module.

forward and cannot be accessed at random. The capability in itself, however, opens up good possibilities for instruction, particularly in language and reading instruction.

Like many of its competitors, Atari has limited offerings in courseware but, like Texas Instruments, has undertaken an active product acquisition campaign. Because of their unique features, it is certain that both the Atari and the TI 99/4 will be competitive in schools in the very near future.

Further development of computer technology offers exciting possibilities for the future. Probably the most exciting application of technology is the linking of computers to videotape and videodisk devices. Beginning with this development, the possibilities become almost endless. The videodisk resembles a 33 rpm record made of aluminum. Data on videodisk can be stored on two sides and are accessed using a laser scanner or a stylus. About 54,000 video frames can be stored on each side which provides 30 minutes in linear play and 60 minutes of motion in constant linear velocity mode. It also has up to four audio channels. An average disk can store about 7.5 million characters of computer data. This is probably sufficient space to store a good portion of an entire encyclopedia *on one side*!

The videodisk can randomly access any video frame in less than 2.5 seconds as well as provide slow motion, stop action, rapid scan, and dual audio. With this capability, it is easy to see why linking videodisk technology to computers offers such incredible possibilities for instruction. One such application has been in interactive television. In this mode, an event is recorded from a number of various angles and recorded on videodisk. The viewer, then, can access with a microcomputer any of these views within seconds and view an event, a procedure, or demonstration over and over from a variety of angles. Imagine, for example, being able to view a football game from any of six camera angles at will. One could see a play from several views as well as see who was in the stands and what was happening on the bench. The videodisk would also allow magnification of any shot so that we could zoom in on any event and see it close up or at a distance. While this football game example represents a rather trivial application, the potential for scientific and medical education, police and industrial training, and many other possibilities gets somewhat overwhelming.

Other plans for networking computer facilities over television cables, telephone lines, and satellite communications hold promise for computer communication networks being brought directly into our homes. With energy becoming more expensive this could mean more people will use their homes as work places, especially in professions where humans interface with machines most of the day. Clerical help who spend most of their day typing can use computers as word processors and probably not need to travel to an office, at least not every day. Computer programmers are already considering using terminals placed in their homes for work instead of traveling to a central office or work place.

Space does not permit a description of all the potential uses of computers. One thing is certain, however. Computers and computers linked with other machines and media will have a great impact on our lives and the lives of our children. As educators we must take the advice of Alvin Toffler (1974) who writes:

> Education springs from the interplay between the individual and a changing environment . . . [we must] help learners cope with real-life crises, opportunities and perils . . . [we must] strengthen the individual's practical ability to anticipate and adapt to change. . . . It is a prime task of education to enhance this ability, to help make the individual more sensitively responsive to change. *We must, therefore, redefine learning itself.*

There is little question that computer technology is already beginning to redefine the way schooling will be conducted. Whether they will redefine the nature of learning itself remains to be seen. In the meantime, as educators we must help learners understand the nature of computers, how they work, and what they can be used for. Those who will inherit the future must be prepared to deal with it.

REFERENCES

Caldwell, R. M. *Introduction to computer-based education.* Minneapolis: Control Data Education Company, 1978.

Caldwell, R. M., & Rizza, P. J. A computer-based system of reading instruction for adult non-readers. *AEDS Journal,* Summer 1979, *12*, 4.

Toffler, A. (Ed.). *Learning for tomorrow.* New York: Vintage Books, 1974.

THE IMPACT OF COMPUTERIZATION ON CHILDREN'S TOYS AND GAMES

Paula Smith, PhD

ABSTRACT. The computer age is not a sudden occurrence; it is a slowly building event of some magnitude. We turn around and realize that we are in the midst of technological greatness. Industry has made the machine palatable and has packaged it in consumer-sized portions at consumer-sized prices. Computers have become such an integral part or our existence that we have developed computers for our children to play with. We have also created an overwhelming number of computerized toys.We must insure that we do not create toys which are brighter than the children whom they are supposed to entertain. What is needed is a modicum of realism. We are in the computer age, and we must adapt, but we can bend it to the human will for the human good.

Rise of the Computer

The computer age is not a sudden occurrence; it is a slowly building event of some magnitude. We turn around and realize that we are in the midst of technological greatness. Often we take for granted the fact that we have "arrived" in relatively short order and fairly painlessly at that. Maybe this is the reason that the existence of computerization in our daily lives dawns on us rather than shocks us. It is perhaps more surprising to realize that only 100 years ago we were without use of electricity as a power source. This period represents an evolutionary

Paula Smith is a child psychologist with Fisher-Price Toys, Department of Research and Development, 636 Girard Avenue, East Aurora, NY 14052.

Journal of Children in Contemporary Society, Vol. 14(1), Fall 1981

drop in the bucket and yet is as responsible for substantially changing our life styles as was the implementation of iron tools in place of stone.

Contributions significant to the creation of computers and computerized products are staggering in their importance independent of these and individually to society. Included are the discovery of electricity; the development of sound harnessed to travel through telegraph, telphone cable, and radio. The combination of these and reconstructed picture images marked the advent of television. People who had grown up with only radio were just getting used to the incomprehensible idea of the picture tube when we found that we could get clear, full-color pictures from all over the world via space satellite—then we were precipitously greeted by television from the moon!

We saw movies about computers which emphasized our limited knowledge and which awakened our secret fears. We had questions about whether or not we could insure our control over computers. We became engrossed in films of computerized warfare where we as humans no longer could decide our strategy—a message to us all. Various accomplishments in computerization began to have direct effects on our lives; they infiltrated the ranks at a very basic level. For a time they aided us in our jobs, then while we were not looking, some of us were replaced by computerized machines; we knew that the time of the computer was upon us. Our work was being performed by inanimate objects. It becomes frightening to think that one's productivity, perhaps one's training for a lifetime, can be replicated, sometimes more efficiently, by a machine. Such is the case in many universities where wonderful elderly ladies used to help students during registration. The ladies filled out your course cards, recommended alternative courses, showed you the ropes. But projections for cost, computers versus ladies, suggested that it was in the best interests of the university to switch to computer-based selections. In one instance the pressure was so great to return to the original plans that the university rehired half of the registration staff and trained them in the use of the computer—not so that they could help the students register, but rather to educate them in how to use the machines so that they *could* register. Such has often been the case in industry and craft; not only are we automated, we are computerized. Fantastic creations in art are done by computer, and most of us probably do not realize it! Look at televised advertisements, drawings for cartoon series which are automated though sometimes slow and photos replicated by computer art. However, there are many instances where these new technological creations have been of great benefit to man. There are medical data banks, help for the precision professional such as industrial engineers, rockets to the moon, logistics at one's fingertips, projects technically free of human error in execution if not in judgment. Many people whose jobs have been replaced are at last free to learn something else; no longer are they bound to automated monotony.

However, there are fears of the unknown, of the power of the machine. The most realistic fear is conjured when we wonder if the computer can be programmed to think logically, and maybe—horror of horrors—in a manner better than humanly possible! We could then be in a position where we might no longer be in control of our destinies.

Computers used to be considered only the tools of the erudite—and indeed they were! One had to know a secret language and complex programs. One had to go to the computer as in the *Wizard of Oz*. They were huge and never portable; they were seen behind locked doors and by appointment only. Cost was prohibitive to owning one and to some for even using one. Computer time was at a premium, and much like the road to Oz, it helped to pay for and justify the machine's existence. We have come a long way even from this in the last 10 years. Industry has made the machine palatable and has packaged it in consumer-sized portions at consumer-sized prices. Remember the transistor radio? They had their day as novelties; they came in every size, shape, style, and color. For a time it was "the smaller the better." Now, although there are still novelty transistor radios on the market, we have come to our senses, and industry has reverted to emphasizing practicality, durability, good tone in spite of size, and we are thankful. The same was attempted with television but certain limitations exist such as with proportionate screen dimensions, and so, although we may go smaller or bigger, we can still recognize a TV.

With computers we have made them smaller and have packaged programs with one-step to multiple instructions. The development of the minute computer chip which can accommodate some of the same kinds of information which the larger computers do has made them available at less expense to the everyday consumer. Many grocery stores are switching to computer cash registers which read information off the product labels. Each label is accorded a price code and so the computer converts the label to a numerical price and thereby avoids much human error—particularly if the store has a large inventory. The nice part is that the cashier has the option of placing fluctuating (e.g., produce) prices in by himself. Yet we were still afraid until we found out that we too could operate simple computers. The pocket calculator has indeed become as popular and as accessible for purchase as a transistor radio. The novelty is still upon us and we find calculator pens, watches, and checkbook balancers.

Yes, we are of the computer age. Any task which can take a numerical representation or which can be converted to computer symbols for computation can become part of a program. It can be as simple as our everyday calculators or as complex as controlled space flight, satellite monitors, and special effects in movies such as *Star Wars*.

Computers have become such an integral part of our existence that we have developed computers for our children to play with. We have also created an overwhelming number of computerized toys. At this point it becomes relevant to make a distinction.

Computer toys are those which have as their main function a completely computerized activity, without which the toy cannot operate. Computerized toys are those which are enhanced in their activities by the provision of a computerized function, but which do not rely solely on the operation of this for the activity of the toy.

Computer Toys Which Are on the Market—What Do They Do?

Toys Which Make Music

There are several toys on the market of this type. For the most part they simulate instruments such as guitar or a one-octave scale "keyboard." "Keys" are colored strips of plastic that lay over a connector that turns on a colored light by touch and coded film switches which allow the child to associate color and tone. As it happens, this association has been found to be one of the best for musical recognition with children—particularly for immediate satisfaction. Experience has shown that mothers are often buying these for children whom they want to encourage to play real instruments. The computer toy versions help to lure them into a field they might not otherwise explore. These are also seen as educational toys by some, while others merely see them as sophisticated noisemakers and would rather stick with pots and pans for the money. The problem, which will be described in detail later, really is one of comprehension for the children. While these musical activities are obviously easier than mastering scales on real instruments, they are also easier then playing with simple band instruments. Because of the electronic limitations, there is sometimes a delayed response in tone after the child pushes the switch. There is rarely a feature built in which can give the child a means of discovering a sense of rhythm. That is, the activity and sound are produced by a machine, not by the child. Indeed, these toys tend to neglect rather than to build musical skills and are limited in their repertoire. These instruments often include a player piano feature, the preprogrammed tunes which one can call up by pressing the correct combination of switches. For adults there are sophisticated music synthesizers which have enormous range and capacity for the generation and replication of sound, but the people who use these normally can play traditional instruments proficiently. Unlike this, the toy instruments appear to encourage shortcuts in play—until we are capable of providing something different.

TV Games

These were the ones you saw first in your local bar, but which were soon made adaptable in a five-game package for your very own television. At the time when these came out, the cost was considered to be prohibitive, but we overcame our inhibitions when we discovered that this was to be the norm as far as cost for computerization.

The first thing one notices is that there seems generally to be manual-audio-visual combinations. TV ping-pong is very simple to learn, difficult to master. It utilizes the aforementioned skills, but it takes a while to realize that we are only seeing and hearing representations, that these are optical and auditory illusions. The paddle does not really hit the ball, nor does the ball really bounce, we do not actually hear either one. The sound is a cue, paired to the visual image so that we are better able to follow the game.

Although these games are nice for a rainy day and may substitute for some TV watching, they are not conducive to group play or interaction.

There is also the fact that many of us, when we think of computers, think of computer noises, clips, and whirrs. What computer game would be complete without computer noise? Our fascination certainly does not end there. These games test our skill against ourselves, time, and a machine. We push ourselves to beat our own scores, since we can play these games with or without a partner.

Arcade Games

We used to see a great deal of pinball, then electronic galleries, mostly with traditional themes. If we visit the local arcade now, we see computerized pinball which scores more efficiently, lights and bells work and work well. But we also see computerized road rallies, submarine fights, cruising asteroids, invaders from outer space, cowboy gunfights. While guns are given the downward thumb, we encourage submarine warfare, computerized destruction of aliens, driving fast without crashing, knocking down walls with speed. It is an interesting commentary when we see youngsters rushing to their local drugstore's single game arcade on Saturday evenings. There they change their dollars to quarters and wait their turns to play each other a game of Space Invaders, for example. There is no talk; all one hears in "Oh!" or "Ach!", etc. When the game is over they shuffle around, still hardly speaking, standing back in line ... waiting, waiting ... for what? They are waiting to be entertained, and we are supporting their passivity.

The Array of Game Toys

There are a plethora of toys in this category, including hand-held, lap, and table versions. There are games of speed, games of sports. Few, if any, encourage us to use our logic. Many are now offering multiple games in one toy.

Games of Speed

Many of these overlap with games of sports in which speed is an essential element. What is common in these games of speed is that the computer sets a speed (sometimes two—fast and faster) and we must perform by pressing buttons.

Musical notes and brightly colored flashing lights are incorporated in some of the games. The object here is to remember the random sequence which the computer provides a note at a time, increasing the number of notes/flashes with each successive turn. In some models the speed increases with each turn so that all notes in one turn are packed into the time equivalent of the first turn. Others have smaller ends, less differentiation between colors for light. These are the most difficult because of the lack of double (distinctive auditory and visual) cueing. This toy enhances auditory and visually sequenced memory skills, but it becomes very quickly apparent that one cannot outlast the computer. Indeed, one can hardly keep up with it.

Another similar game toy provides the full tonal sequence beginning with several notes (the number being of your choice) and asks you to repeat them. If you do not complete it correctly, you receive the "computer raspberry." Fortunately, this game comes as a part of a series, and we do not always have to play just that one.

The arcade space game was scaled down and now we have a hand-held version which challenges our eyesight and our reaction time. It is difficult as an adult to get used to the multiple action as well as the amateur (as opposed to pro) speed of this game. One has to protect one's spaceship behind one of two forts which can be destroyed by a litter of small spaceships. Included is a mother ship which moves across the top of the screen and in alternating directions. In order to get points, one must first survive attack and then retaliate by shooting at the small ships. If one hits the mother ship before being destroyed, he or she can get bonus points. Speed of the small space ships moving across the screen increases when only two are left. In addition, the ships move closer each time they come across in a random pattern from left to right or vice-versa. At any one time there may be as many as 10 moving lights accompanied by appropriate hit, score, or loss beeps. The amazing thing is that one can, in time, accommodate to the speed and range of activity. This toy exemplifies what can be put into one simple program and the complexity with which we have begun to deal in the regular market place.

Games of Sports

One of the first, and best loved, computer games is that of football. The game simulates the sport as far as the field, points, and object. At first it is really quite difficult to "see" what one is supposed to do. However, this becomes clear with repetitions; the real game begins. It is very fast and involves spatial perceptions, player decision, and quick (eye-finger) reflexes. It provides an element of surprise, and it also lets you win occasionally, unlike some.

Tic-tac-toe, although not a sport, is a good computer game because the computer cannot lose. This is one of the more frustrating elements of these games. The program for tic-tac-toe is not very complex, and there is only a limited range of options with which the computer must deal. There is, in fact, no way for the player to win except possibly in a new dimension. So, we have a built-in draw or failure factor which is not the best type of play with which to confront anyone, least of all a child.

There are many other sport games such as baseball, soccer, etc. They are generally based upon the same principles of speed, a simple but fast decision, luck, and fast reflexes. One even teaches your child how to play roulette, and another plays "21."

What features do all of these computer toys have in common?

1. We play on the game's terms—as we do in all games, but these are without option.
2. We search *our* memory banks and scan *our* digital information systems in order to compete on the same level.
3. We use eye-thumb or eye-finger coordination. The time of the eye-hand coordination for these games is past.
4. There are few speed settings, and they are preset.
5. There are both light and noise features.
6. There is rarely a second chance.
7. The player rarely wins.
8. Some do not have well-defined limits. No matter how far along the player can go, the toy's program can take it further, better, and faster. There is no mastery.
9. Age appropriateness is questionable at best, both due to developmental level and skill emphasis.
10. They are two dimensional illusions.

What About Children?

Novelty

Children love novel items; they stimulate their curiosity and excite the imagination. They invite exploration and play. As they get older, some of their toys require sophistication and must be realistic; others are of a more abstract nature, and they can manipulate their creativity at will. They play games with each other, and they play games alone. Computer games are interesting in the aspect of socialization. Children take their toy to school, and it makes one quite popular. The problem is that everyone wants to play with the new game rather than with you. Children invite their friends over to play with their toys rather than with themselves; it is even evident in their communication.

In a society that stresses individuality and independence, are we going a bit too far—encouraging, through play, an isolationist approach?

On the other hand, many children go home to sit passively in front of the television set. Would we rather have them playing "computer" games?

After the novelty wears off, children become skilled at the various games, and, surprisingly, unlike many of their other toys, they come back to some of the computer games again and again. The appeal is in the fact that there is no mastery, and yet they are held on the edges of their seats. They want to try it just one more time, much as we succumb to the lure of carnival games.

Are These Games Constructed?

Yes, some are, but for the most part there is little involved vis-à-vis goal-directed activity and emphasis on skills, with the exception of those mentioned before. They are playing in two dimensions while operating in three. They are not taught to think better; they are not really taught to approach something differently, only on another plane. Yet these games stimulate the child; that is their biggest contribution. In a society where the televison screen is of prime importance, children look at their miniature screens, and they can entertain themselves by lifting only a finger.

Man' inventions have always been an extension of himself, particularly of his hands (such as pliers, tweezers, etc.) What we have now is the extension of man's brain, and it is awesome. We have developed complex systems and games which were never before possible, and we are only beginning to tap our own resourcefulness.

Where do the difficulties lie regarding child development? What are the limitations in application?

We must insure that we do not create toys which are brighter than the children whom they are supposed to entertain. We must be careful that children are encouraged through appropriate developmental steps such as sensory, motor, and perceptual tasks. Even though today's children may be more precocious and more sophisticated in their thinking than yesteryear's children, we cannot afford to overwhelm them with such heady stuff, particularly in their early development years. We risk their not ever being able to come to grips with their evolutionary heritage. Man came to where he is through the use of his hands; we cannot afford to let them lose this to symbolic digits.

Specifically, everything is built-in; there is nothing the child can do to "render" it. These toys are mechanical and rob the child of his imagination. He/she cannot see how the toy works; in fact, on most of the toys, there is a warning that the backs should not be opened.

The movement which is generated in cartoons and which makes them believable and appealing to children is the same type as the attention-catching movement in computer toys. The problem lies in the fact that young children (cartoon age) have an animistic way of looking at this movement. Although the toy is man-made, the child perceives that it has a life of its own, that essentially it has a primitive "brain" (although they certainly cannot state it in these terms!).

Additionally, there are difficulties in industry. How do we insure the age appropriateness of a "mind" toy when we are not even sure how the mind works? We can observe skill levels and watch how children play and how they learn, but we must be very careful.

For the most part, although many traditionally male sports are the subjects of computer toys, they transcend the stigma of sexism and this is a great plus.

What of Our Great Mores?

If we allow that we are in the age of computers, can we also allow "reading, writing, and calculators?" We are heading in that direction. Many children are using calculators instead of learning their math. If calculators are here to stay, do they need to learn $2 + 2 = 4$ when they can just plug it in?

Tradition really is *the* question. Can we overcome ourselves? Perhaps, but with moderation. Children eventually move on to other things; right now they are returning to real musical instruments and toys which they can manipulate such as construction toys, blocks, realistic figures which simulate their daydreams. It is as if they took too great a bite of the cheesecake and asked instead to have a hamburger and fries next time. Let us not encourage nonproductivity.

Computers in the classroom are a great boost to teaching, but cannot replace teachers. When asked who the three most important and influential figures in one's life are, most people mention at least one parent and a teacher. Can you imagine mentioning "computer 3RXFZ" instead?

The Horizon

Must man's reach exceed his grasp? Yes, of course; but we need not be propelled into precipitous developments when we have the time and the skill for in-depth examinations. We must now reach with our hands and our minds to overcome limitations in application.

Although the computer may learn finally how to play chess quite well, in order to replicate the human brain it is estimated that it would take 10 blocks of buildings 10 stories high of micro-units. That means duplicating the function at least 10 billion neurons, and even then no one is sure it can be done. Yet we are right to have some fear; 1984 is creeping up on us. We are already a somewhat alienated society and are in danger of robotizing ourselves. There is even computer crime, involving accounts of stocks, etc. It is at its peak, and there is a government agency which was developed just to deal with this.

What is needed is a modicum of realism. We are in the computer age, and we must adapt, but we can bend it to the human will for the human good. Children need to be socialized and encouraged to learn and perform at their own levels. We should not pass them by, but help them and provide tools, not mechanical crutches or substitutes.

> Computers are used in many seemingly different ways in modern life, to the point that they are frequently misnamed "electronic brains." Although the amount of work performed by the computer and the man together is much greater than could have been performed by the man alone, the type of work that has been done could have been performed, in principle, by the man. *He* has to *organize* it in any case. (Gear, 1973)

REFERENCE

Gear, C. W. *Introduction to computer science*. Chicago: Science Research Associates, Inc., 1973.

A LEARNING AID:
IMAGINATIVE ELECTRONICS
APPLIED TO EDUCATION

Barbara Thompson, MEd, PhD
Theresa Cloer, MA

ABSTRACT. Computer technology continues to make inroads into the educational environment with such new products as electronic hand-held learning aids. Texas Instruments, one of the leaders in this area, takes education seriously enough to make sure that each learning aid produced has an educational objective and that the product meets this objective in a positive manner. With the guidance of a new discipline called "learning factors engineering," educators and engineers work together to ensure the educational validity and value of a learning aid. At Texas Instruments, learning aids are electronic products that: (1) are designed around educational objectives, (2) are built to provide motivation and appeal for the user, (3) do not simply present information, (4) evaluate responses and provide immediate and positive feedback, (5) present valid and valuable information.

Hal, the talking computer, was an unrealized fantasy when *2001* hit the movie screens in the '60s, as was space travel when Buck Rogers blasted off every Sunday morning in his cartoon strip. Today, talking computers and space travel are realities. Computer technology, a dream of yesteryear, has begun to play an ever increasing role in our everyday lives. It has grown to affect our lifestyles, our standard of living, and even our children's education.

Barbara Thompson is Educational Software Development Specialist, P.O. Box 225012, M/S 84, Texas Instruments, Dallas TX 75265. Theresa Cloer is Educational Product Support Manager at Texas Instruments.

Journal of Children in Contemporary Society, Vol. 14 (1), Fall 1981
© 1982 The Haworth Press

The classroom environment is just beginning to feel the effects of computer technology. Barriers which once impeded the application of computers to education are being eliminated. Improvements in the efficiency and quality of the computer, refinements in design, and decreased costs have made computer technology more and more inviting to educators. More important than the improvement of the technology is the realization by educators that the interactive nature of the computer itself enhances learning. When working with a computer, the student can do much more than simply act as a passive recipient of information. Computers invite active participation.

The computer's delivery-discovery system has a variety of applications in education. Drill and practice, tutorial instruction, games, simulations, and problem-solving can all be part of a classroom computer system. Computer-aided instruction (CAI) and computer-managed instruction (CMI) on large time-sharing systems have found their niche in the classroom alongside minicomputers, microcomputers, and calculators. Hand-held learning aids, one of the newest outgrowths of computer technology, have only begun to make their appearance on the educational scene.

As some of the newest by-products of computer technology, learning aids are in a class by themselves. They are, by definition, electronic learning devices designed to complement and supplement typical classroom instruction. Learning aids can individualize instruction for learners while providing positive reinforcement and motivation. They can even help lengthen a child's attention span or the time spent on a given task. Learning aids are for all learners. They provide practice for remedial students and challenge for the gifted. Learning aids are the link between yesterday's proven learning theories, today's learner, and tomorrow's world. A child's interaction with a learning aid can familiarize him with computer technology and speed him toward a place in time where society is "computer comfortable."

In a world replete with video games and hand-held sports games, a Texas Instruments learning aid competes only with itself. The staff of the TI Learning Center continually works to increase the gap between electronic games and the Texas Instruments' line of learning aids. Frequently the distinction is clouded, but close examiniation of the underlying design of both learning aids and games reveals concept differences. The primary goal of electronic learning aids is to use available technologies in the fulfillment of educational objectives. Fun and entertainment are the natural results of a positive learning experience rather than the only result.

Driving the development of all Texas Instruments learning aids is a discipline termed "learning factors engineering." Like "human factors engineering," which is also applied to learning aids, learning factors engineering provides guidelines for determining *how* a person learns with a machine. Human factors analyzes the physical interaction between man and machine, while learning factors delves into the mental interaction between these two entities. In short, what human factors is to the body, learning factors is to the mind.

At the heart of learning factors engineering is the belief that the learner's first contact with an electronic product requires an immediate response followed by a positive interaction. For this reason, all TI learning aids encourage the learner to get involved the minute the ON button is pressed. Speak & Spell prompts the learner to "Spell" a word. Little Professor gives the child a problem to solve. Then, the electronic learning aid provides a motivating response to whatever answer the learner gives. The synthesized voice of Speak & Spell rewards correct answers with "That's right. Now try. . . ." DataMan's response to a correct answer is a light show in the display. The devices' responses to incorrect answers are designed to encourage, not discourage, the learner. To insure against frustration, most learning aids allow the learner a second opportunity to respond correctly before providing the correct answer.

Texas Instruments learning aids:

—are designed around educational objectives.
—are built to provide motivation and appeal for the user.
—require interaction between product and learner rather than simply presenting information.
—appropriately reinforce correct responses.
—evaluate responses and provide immediate and positive feedback to the learner.
—present valid and valuable information to the learner.

Texas Instruments' learning aids are designed to enhance a student's progress in subject areas that are normally part of a preschool, elementary, secondary, or college curriculum and to add value to what is being taught in the classroom. To ensure that a learning aid is both valid and valuable, products must have specific educational objectives. For example, the primary objective of Speak & Spell is to provide the opportunity for an elementary-age child of average ability to practice spelling. Engineers and educators designed the primary operation, Spell It, to accomplish this objective. Speak & Spell's other operational modes enhance the primary objective.

Learning aids must survive in the same family room with Saturday morning cartoons. Inherent to this situation is another challenge: provide the learner with a variety of learning options. Today's learners are accustomed to, and expect, freedom of choice. This expectation must be met for a learning aid to be successful, and this freedom must apply to learning alternatives. For example, TI's newest talking learning aid Speak & Read utilizes several widely accepted learning theories to teach beginning readers while keeping its main objective: facilitate the reading process for the beginner. Speak & Read is designed to provide the learner the opportunity to practice sight recognition of words, comprehension, and vocabulary building. It also aids phonic development by allowing children to build word families.

The technical aspects of a product's design are also weighed according to high educational standards. For example, if a new technology such as synthesized speech is to be utilized in a learning aid, great care is taken to ensure that the speech is appropriate and understandable. What a product says and when it says it are of the utmost importance in the consideration of a design for a talking learning aid. The voices of Speak & Spell, Speak & Read, and Speak & Math are natural, as well as instructive, and positive in what they say to a learner. Great care is taken to control the quality of each word and sound so that a learner does not have two obstacles to overcome: (1) responding correctly to the activity and (2) understanding the words.

A learning aid is not complete, however, until its operational scenarios and educational objectives are reviewed by nationally recognized authorities in education. These educators, whether classroom teachers or college professors, bring to product design a knowledge of practical education. They are teachers and theorists dedicated to quality education on a daily basis, and their recommendations and contributions to product design are greated valued. Texas Instruments' concern for the quality of learning aids demands more than ability and experience from its consultants; TI demands vision. As a result, TI consultants are those individuals who can see that electronics applied to education is the wave of the future.

Because learning aids are part of the future world, they have a unique position in today's world. They must not only continue to meet the needs of today's students but foresee the needs of tomorrow's. The task is not to provide a new medium for time-proven educational approaches, but to create the best transitional medium, one with the flexibility to adapt to tomorrow's educational requirements.

Learning aids can provide today's learner with the impetus to learn. A Speak & Read or a Little Professor only begins the learning process by providing the child with an entertaining way to practice the basics of reading, mathematics, or spelling. A TI learning aid package takes this process one step farther. Colorful activity books accompany each product and give the learner an opportunity to apply newly acquired skills. Through repeated application, these skills can be internalized to complete the learning cycle.

Although learning aids and activity books can enhance the learning experience, human interaction is still a necessary component. Parent and teacher interaction with the learner reinforces the learning process. To help parents become more involved in this process, parents' guides accompanying each learning aid provide detailed information about the product. In addition, these guides furnish information about how parents can best work with their children to enrich the interaction between child and learning aid. Learning aids are designed to complement the learning process; they are not designed to replace the teacher or parent. These learning devices provide the teacher with yet another medium with which to convey a concept. The unique and independent operation of the electronic learning aid can free the teacher to provide the element which no machine can—the warmth and personal encouragement that only another human being can bring to the learning experience.

Learning aids are only the beginning of a world of technologies designed to assist the learner. Inevitably, as technologies are advancing, so are learning devices. Their applications are extending:

—to a variety of learners—the gifted, handicapped, remedial, adults, toddlers, and the bilingual.
—in a myriad of subject areas—the sciences, the social sciences, the language arts.
—in a variety of settings—the home, the classroom, or continued education programs.

Uses and applications of computer technology to education are limited only by mankind's imagination and creativity.

COMPUTER-BASED EDUCATION
IN THE AGE OF NARCISSISM

John E. Searles, EdD

ABSTRACT. To many observers, the world is entering a new age with the advent of electronic communication technology, particularly television and computers. This mental revolution will probably cause as many changes as did the industrial revolution; mental energy will be extended as physical energy has been extended.

These changes will come to all societies, developed and underdeveloped. One of the effects could be that schools will lose their predominant place in society and will change from a function of presenting information to that of organizing information. Beyond this we can only speculate on the effect of computer-based education in the Age of Narcissism.

The culture of modern America, according to many observers, is characterized by a quality of narcissism, a name derived from the ancient Greek myth of the young man who spent hours gazing at his own reflection in the still waters of a pool. This sense of introspection and examination of the self is bothersome to these observers as they wonder what happens to the common good in a society whose individuals look inwards upon themselves. Labelling them the "Me Generation," the critics may also recall that Narcissus also became a symbol of death, and, to them, the present narcissism can be the death of society.

Previous articles in this issue have alluded to a revolutionary technology which will have a marked impact on this culture. These deep and wrenching changes, which may be called a mental revolution, are the

John E. Searles is Professor of Education, The Pennsylvania State University, 146 Chambers Building, University Park, PA 16820.

Journal of Children in Contemporary Society, Vol. 14(1), Fall 1981

result of an expanding and increasingly sophisticated information technology.

So the young children living in this narcissistic culture are standing on a threshold of a new era. Will this revolution reinforce the narcissism or will our culture throw off the preoccupation with self-examination? Will the young children grow up to examine and admire themselves in the stream of life or will they enter it and splash about with more vigor? Although the metaphor might be overly vivid, it is a matter of concern and well worth examination. So let us look at that culture and at information technology and then speculate on the impacts that technology might have on children in the narcissistic age.

The Modern Narcissus

We are living in a culture that may have plenty of reasons to cause this introspection that characterizes our times. The first and foremost characteristic is that we are living in a postindustrial society. We are living at the end of a revolution which has tremendously increased the amount of physical energy available to each human being. Humans in the industrialized societies of the world are generally liberated from the tedium of the daily tasks of providing for the basic needs of food, shelter, clothing, and transportation. The products of the industrial age, the machines, do this for them.

But, as humans look at the prospects for survival in the postindustrial world, they begin to see that the prospects may be dismal. The industrial revolution has polluted the environment. Air in the cities causes diseases, rivers are so polluted that they become fire hazards, lakes and beaches become so polluted that poeple cannot swim. Our industrial power has increased our power for destruction as we continue to produce armaments when we already have enough power to kill all of the people in the world several times. The current arsenal of nuclear weapons that is aimed and ready to fire is estimated to have the destructive power of thousands of the bombs that ushered in the atomic age in 1945.

We face a continuing crisis in this postindustrial world of getting enough energy to fuel our desires. Another very important product of the postindustrial culture is that because we have produced so many material goods, the individual has a massive confusion between needs and wants. The wants and desires of a few years ago have become our present needs. Although the luxuries of past generations have become necessities to present generations, we continue to increase the number of products and increase the desire for those products. So the number of needs increases.

But the prospect for the future that seems to have the most influence on the young people in our culture comes from the changes in family life and the changes in family structures. We have developed and are using a technology which makes it possible to control the number of births. As a result of this power of decision, the American society is undergoing a period of lowering birth rates. Consequently, school districts which used to have to build school buildings rapidly to take care of the incoming population are now selling those very buildings because the number of children entering school is diminishing every year. The second point is that more and more families have both parents at work. It is estimated that over 60% of the American women of child-bearing age are at work. The repercussions on the rearing and education of children have yet to be measured but we do have to face the fact that the women are changing their image from that of being mother and mother only to sharing that interest with interests outside the family, primarily in the work force. Another characteristic of the modern family life is the growth in the number of single parents, parents who have chosen to rear children by themselves. A final characteristic that we must take into account is the phenomenon of the graying of America. As more people have turned the corner toward being middle-aged and elderly the attention of American society is focused on them with the consequent diminishing of interest in the younger people. So the result of this phenomenon of the changing family structures seems to be that the society is not quite so child centered as it once was.

The Mental Revolution

As we turn from this postindustrial time, we look to a future in which there is a new revolution that might be called the mental revolution. A technology of information has been developed in using television and computers hooked together in ways which will revolutionize our lives. To discuss these in any detail would only repeat previous articles. However, it might be well to examine computer-based education, a highly sophisticated form of information technology and then examine its impact on the educational process.

Computer-based education has several characteristics which separate it from any other information technology. First, computers are able to store vast amounts of information. The amount of information is limited only by the size of the memory of the computers. New information technology of the videodisc will expand this capability even further. Videodiscs, the size of the current audiodiscs, can be programmed to have as much information as 100 volumes of books, and these discs will, it is estimated, cost around $10 apiece.

A second characteristic of computers in education is that the computers can retrieve this vast amount of information in almost any order, and furthermore, they can retrieve this information by the command of either the learner or by a programmed set of instructions that have been built into the computer. Contrast this with the book. A book, as an information storage mechanism, contains information in the form of words, placed in an order that is impossible to change once the book is printed. To find one's way through that information and retrieve any of the information takes a great deal of time and familiarity with the total book. On the other hand, a computer containing the same amount of information can retrieve parts of that information by obeying the command of either the learner or instructions previously programmed into the machine.

Another characteristic of computer-based education is that the computer is able to use two different systems of symbolic expression. It is necessary here to pause to describe these two systems. One system might be called "analogic." Analogic symbols are a direct representation of reality. A model of the world in the form of a map is an analogic symbol. A photo of the President of the United States is an analogic symbol. Pictures, printed in sequence so that they can be projected in a way that makes them look as if the objects move, are also analogic symbols. The use of this analogic symbol has been brought to new heights by that information technology known as television.

Another set of symbols can be called a digital system of symbolic representation. Digital symbols are highly abstract. There is no direct correspondence to reality: they are abstractions from it.

We have devoted most of our school teaching to the use of digital symbols. We teach students the use of words; we teach them how to abstract the meaning from words in programs that we call reading. We sum it all up by saying a word is worth a thousand pictures.

And we turn it around and say a picture is worth a thousand words. We have a finite number of words to represent an infinite number of objects and thoughts. So even with precision in the meaning of digital symbols we find that the symbols can be worth many pictures.

Up until now, our information technology has pretty much had to choose between the analogic or the digital. The computer with its access to information storage devices and its ability to retrieve information of all types will enable us to mix the two of them.

Impacts of Technology

This technology of information technology and computer-based education will have impacts that are going to change schooling, learners, and whole societies in ways we cannot imagine. We feel with Horatio hearing Hamlet declare that there is more to heaven and earth than dreamed in our philosophy. We can sketch out a few of these and shudder at the idea of reading these 10 years from now when we will wonder at our glorious innocence.

Impacts on the Schools

The first and obvious impact will be made by the use of the machines. The machines are just that—machines; they are not gods. They are not human. They are tools, excellent and sophisticated, which will enable the schools to be better.

If we find that machines can present information better than the teachers, we can use the machines to present that information and free the teacher to do the far more sophisticated intellectual tasks of organizing a massive amount of information and evaluate the attainment of that information.

A second change in the school is that the schools can shift to a higher intellectual level. The lower intellectual levels of memorization of information and the evaluation of that memorization by repetition can be left to the computer. On the other hand, the teacher can work with the students at the higher intellectual levels of analysis, synthesis and a genuine judgment.

Another characteristic of the school in this new age of the computer would be that the teacher would be liberated to work as a humane being. Instead of dealing with the routines of the presentation of knowledge, the teacher will be able to work at the human levels dealing with students as humans, their values, their interests, their dreams, their emotions.

A final change in the schooling will be that there will be a growing emphasis in the skill of making individual decisions using information. The product of information will be in second place to the process of the use of the information. The schools will be teaching how to use computers to store their own information, to retrieve information that they need and to use that information to make decisions that are necessary.

Impacts on the Individual

All of these changes in the schools will mean, of course, changes in the individuals who attend the schools. The first change will be a change toward more liberation. The student will be confronted with more choices. The learner of the future will not be sitting at a desk with 30 other students in a room in front of a teacher listening to voices. Instead, that learner will be sitting at a keyboard with the computer screen with videodiscs inputs, with books, with other forms of information technology at the fingertips ready to use. The directions and inspiration for the use of these will come from the human being, the teacher.

Another change in the individual will result from a change in our society as the society moves toward fuller use of information technology. Alvin Toffler in his book *The Third Wave* speaks of one of the major effects of this new age as the "electronic cottage." He estimates that in most occupations 30–40% of the work can be done away from the headquarters of the commerical establishment. As our energy to transport the physical body diminishes we will, says Toffler, have developed communication networks between houses that will allow people to stay at home and communicate with one another and their offices by the use of electronic devices. The home with its home computer, telephone lines, networks of television, information will be more of the center of life. The electronic cottage will allow people, in Toffler's phrase, to "telecommute" rather than physically commute. This will change family structures and, in turn, change the individual in the school.

Impacts on Society

However, the biggest impact of this computer-based education will be on the society. The society and the schools will have to face the fact that there will be no one institution designed to educate the young. For centuries in our civilizations the education of the young took place in an institution that we have known as the family. During the industrial revolution with its growth in specialization, we developed an institution to educate children which we called the "school." In the last 10 years we have found that students spend more time in another institution between the ages 5 and 16 than they do in school or with the family. The attendance to the electronic media of television and radio is estimated to be more than 30% higher than the attendance at school or with the family. To this we add, the coming information technology called the computer. As computers come to more and more homes, as computers are linked together to more sophisticated networks that can bring them more and more information, as information storage centers are developed, it will be entirely possible to have students spend more time in front of computers than in front of the school teacher or in front of television. The school will have to recognize that it is no longer the central educational institution for the youth.

The effects of new information technology have been noted on the "culture of Narcissus." It must be emphasized that not all cultures in our world are caught in this pattern. To the cultures of the Third World the new technologies can be a means to solving one of the most pressing of their problems: education of the young. In these cultures—and they encompass a majority of the world's population—35 to 45% of the population is under 18 years of age.

The problems of educating this mass are staggering. One solution may be that these new technologies may allow the necessary expansion of educational power. These cultures may create new institutions; schools may have different functions as they coordinate the technologies for education, or schools as we have known them might not be built.

To paraphrase H. G. Wells (with a little Chaplin) "Modern times are a race between education and catastrophe." Modern technologies can be used on the side of education. It might not be too much to wish that they will be so used.

Conclusion

So it would seem that the repercussions of the computer on this Age of Narcissism put those of us in education at a crossroads. The computer can be a liberating technology, freeing teachers and students alike, or if our experience with television is any guide, it will be a pacifying institution allowing, permitting, urging students to be quiescent and not participate at all in their learning. The choice seems to be ours at this time.

This choice is summed up by two quotations from books which give an excellent background for teachers standing at these crossroads.

The pessimistic road that can be taken is presented by Christopher Lasch (1979) in *The Culture of Narcissism*: "Universal public education, instead of creating a community of self-governing citizens, has contributed to the spread of intellectual torpor and political passivity" (p. 229).

The more optimistic view is expressed by Christopher Evans (1980) in *The Micro Millennium:*

> concerted efforts will be made to ensure that. . . teaching computers sell to *every* child. To achieve this the computers and the programs they offer will be carefully prepared to make sure that the user at whatever intellectual or cultural level, will be motivated to use them. . . . the world is about to move on from the era where knowledge comes locked up in devices known as books, knowledge which can be released once the keys to their use have been acquired. In the [coming] era, the books will come down from their shelves, unlock and release their contents, and cajole, even beseech, their owners to make use of them (pp. 128–129).

To paraphrase Frost, which will be the road not taken?

REFERENCES

Evans, C. The micro millennium. New York: Viking, 1980, p. 128-129.
Lash, C. The culture of narcissism. New York: W.W. Norton, 1979, p. 229.
Toffler, A. The third wave. New York: Morrow, 1980